The Art Institute of Chicago

100 MASTERPIECES

The Art of Chic

100

Institute

ago

MASTERPIECES

THE ART INSTITUTE OF CHICAGO

Distributed by Rand McNally & Company/Printed by R. R. Donnelley & Sons Company

Editor and Coordinator: Janice J. Feldstein
Co-editor: Maureen Smith
Designer: Chris Arvetis
Research Assistant: Mary Kuzniar

Color separations, printing, and binding
by R. R. Donnelley & Sons Company, The Lakeside Press,
Crawfordsville, Indiana

Design and composition
by Rand McNally & Company, Chicago, Illinois

Printed on 100# Lustro Offset Enamel Gloss
by S. D. Warren Company, Chicago, Illinois

The illustration on the dust jacket is a detail of
The Millinery Shop, *by Edgar Degas, c. 1882.*
The full painting is reproduced on page 108–109.
The end papers are an enlargement of a detail
from The Millinery Shop.

First printing
Library of Congress Catalogue Card Number: 78-56322

PRINTED IN THE UNITED STATES OF AMERICA

Foreword

IN CELEBRATION OF its distinguished 100-year history, The Art Institute of Chicago has chosen 100 masterpieces of painting representative of the great art treasures that it holds in trust.

This book is sponsored by the Auxiliary Board of The Art Institute. It is a tribute to the discerning patrons and private collectors who contribute to the Institute as well as to the professionals and Trustees who administer its funds and preserve its magnificent collections.

The words "representative" and "treasures" inevitably raise questions about the criteria for selecting 100 paintings. Our aim has been to present a balanced representation of the diversity and strengths of the Art Institute's painting collection. Our sampler here, arranged roughly in chronological order, presents notable examples of Western painting. It inevitably reflects the tastes and interests of the Institute's benefactors and staff. Rather than make a critical statement, the main purpose of this book is to give pleasure to its readers.

While the color plates will suggest the richness and superlative quality of the Institute's holdings, the introductory text will paint a portrait of a major American institution—its history, the development of its facilities, its place within the dynamic city it serves, and the benefactors and supporters past and present who have enabled The Art Institute of Chicago to achieve its position of eminence.

We hope the book will refresh the memories of you who have been fortunate enough to visit here and bring the Institute into the homes of others who have not yet had that opportunity. In either case, it is an invitation to see—or to see again—the originals.

James W. Alsdorf
Chairman
The Art Institute of Chicago

Acknowledgements

A PUBLICATION such as this reflects the efforts of many minds and hands. As a treasury of representative works from the Art Institute's painting collection, this book is, of course, a tribute to the leadership and dedication of several recent Presidents and Chairmen of the Board—Chauncey McCormick, Everett D. Graff, William McCormick Blair, Frank H. Woods, Leigh B. Block, and James W. Alsdorf. Special recognition must go to The Auxiliary Board of The Art Institute of Chicago, which conceived the idea for commemorating the Centennial of the Institute in this way and which has been responsible for the planning and execution of this book through the administrations of its three presidents, Thomas E. Keim, Michael Goodkin, and David C. Hilliard.

Thanks are also due to Miss Louise Lutz, Corporate Secretary of the Art Institute, who has devotedly served since the early thirties, and whose thorough knowledge of the Institute's history and its collection have been of inestimable help in the preparation of this volume. John Maxon, formerly Vice President for Collections and Exhibitions, helped in the selection of the paintings to be included in this book and prepared preliminary notes for the texts before his untimely death.

Special thanks must be expressed to R. R. Donnelley & Sons and to Rand McNally & Company for their deep interest in this book and for the meticulous care they have taken in its production.

Appreciation must be expressed to E. Laurence Chalmers, Jr., President, and to the countless members of the staff of the Art Institute who, as always, have patiently given their time and graciously shared their knowledge.

THE ART INSTITUTE OF CHICAGO

TRUSTEES AND OFFICERS 1977-1978

THE AUXILIARY BOARD OF THE ART INSTITUTE OF CHICAGO 1977-1978

The *America Windows*, by Marc Chagall.
Gift of the City of Chicago and
the Auxiliary Board of the Art Institute.
The six panels represent Music, Painting, Literature,
The Declaration of Independence,
Patriotism, Theatre, and Dance.

CHAGALL
REIMS

Contents

The reconstructed Trading Room from
the old Chicago Stock Exchange Building,
made possible through a generous gift from
the Walter E. Heller Foundation.
The ceiling of the room was made
from fifteen different stencils.

INTRODUCTION

Introduction

Photograph by Chicago Tribune

THE ART INSTITUTE OF CHICAGO was established 100 years ago in a city young and hopeful, far from centers of culture and sophistication but looking with confidence and expectation toward a new and significant future.

Only a few years earlier, in 1871, Chicago was a pile of smoking ruins, its landscape a windswept desolate plain. Perhaps it was the trauma of the Great Fire itself that awakened in some of Chicago's leaders the determination to rebuild a city that would challenge the financial and cultural supremacy of the finest Eastern and European capitals. Not only were they determined that the phoenix would rise—it would rise with vitality, grace, and grandeur.

In 1878, an effort was made to assist the work of the Academy of Design, an institution that had been established by a group of artists in 1866, by adding to the artist membership a board of trustees composed of businessmen. But in the course of a year, new difficulties arose—old debts haunted the efforts of the struggling organization, and questions of policy aroused conflict and frustration. First incorporated May 24, 1879, as the Chicago Academy of Fine Arts, it subsequently, in December 1882, became The Art Institute of Chicago. Charles L. Hutchinson was elected its first president.

Hutchinson had responded to the needs of the fledgling institution with a contribution of fifty dollars—the first installment in what was to be a lifetime of generosity. He was one of the city's most prominent citizens—a member of the Board of Trade, president of the Corn Exchange National Bank, a board member of many of the city's large corporations, trustee of the Chicago Symphony Orchestra, and a trustee and treasurer of the University of Chicago. A pattern was clearly being established. Whereas the great museums of Europe had generally developed from the magnificent collections of royalty or the nobility, museums in the United States were to develop through the beneficence of an extraordinary private patronage.

By the late 1870s other businessmen, as well as Hutchinson, were beginning to have a vision of Chicago's role. The Commercial Club, an organization composed of the leading businessmen in the city, framed the question in one of its monthly programs devoted to a discussion of civic purpose: "Should not the commercial prosperity of great cities be attended by the cultivation of art, literature, science, and comprehensive charities, and the establishment of art museums, public libraries, industrial schools, and free hospitals?"

The acknowledged community leaders were clearly developing a conception of their civic responsibilities that matched that of Boston's merchant families. Such New England overtones were not surprising in a group which had many ties to the East. Art, they believed, played an essential role in the ideal society. Before long their parlors were testimony. "It is more common," wrote a contemporary observer, "to see good engravings in the residences of Chicago than in those of New York."

Chicagoans understood that art was more than just a private matter. It was to be a community resource, supported by the development of a group of citizens who were committed to culture and ready to turn their time and interests toward its realization. The Chicago poet Vachel Lindsay, who considered himself an evangelist carrying on a "warfare for Beauty and Democracy," expressed the sense of mission in a typical turn-of-the-century way:

Go plant the arts that woo the weariest:
Bold arts that simple workmen understand,
That make no poor men and keep all men rich,
And throne our lady Beauty in the land!

THE GROWTH OF THE COLLECTIONS

The Academy of Fine Arts was incorporated May 24, 1879, for "the founding and maintenance of schools of art and design, the formation, and exhibition of collections of objects of art, and the cultivation and extension of the arts of design by any appropriate means." At the time of its incorporation the new institution was located in rented rooms at the southwest corner of State and Monroe Streets. When the name of the Academy was changed to The Art Institute of Chicago, property was purchased on the southwest corner of Michigan Avenue and Van Buren Street for $45,000. John Wellborn Root, a prominent Chicago architect, designed a building in the Romanesque style, which opened in 1887. The building housed the school studios, lecture halls, and galleries for the Chicago Society of Decorative Arts (later to be known as The Antiquarian Society). The ground floor was used for the display of the Elbridge G. Hall collection of plaster casts which formed the core of the Art Institute's early holdings and were intended as a "comprehensive illustration of the whole history of sculpture."

But even with the leasing of two additional floors of the adjoining Studebaker Building (now the Fine Arts Building) the Institute rapidly outgrew its quarters, and again there was discussion of a permanent location. It was suggested that the Institute be moved to Jackson Park, where it would be more convenient and accessible for the city's first families, many of whom then resided in Hyde Park. But the Trustees, headed by Charles Hutchinson, prevailed, and it was decided that the Art Institute should retain its central location.

It was Hutchinson (serving also as chairman of the Committee on Fine Arts of the World's Columbian Exposition of 1893) who had the notion that the Institute could cooperate with the fair's managers in the building of a hall for the World's Congresses which would ultimately revert to the Art Institute as a permanent home. The construction would be financed by a $400,000 sum to be raised by the Trustees to augment the Exposition's budget of $200,000 for a building on Michigan Avenue at Adams Street.

In 1891 a city ordinance was passed authorizing the erection of this building and specifying that it was to be the property of the City of Chicago. The Boston architectural firm of Shepley, Rutan and Coolidge was commissioned to design the building, and construction took place between February 1892 and May 1893 when the Columbian Exposition opened. The World's Congresses closed on October 31, 1893, and scarcely more than a month later, on December 8, The Art Institute of Chicago was opened in the neo-classical quarters on the east side of Michigan Avenue, which it has occupied to the present day.

The new Institute inherited more than a building from the World's Columbian Exposition. It inherited a mood of confidence, a verve, a feeling of role and destiny that was to provide the momentum for the years of steady growth and development that were to come. The fair brought a heady atmosphere to the city: it seemed to serve notice that Chicago had arrived as a cultural center.

From the outset the Art Institute grew swiftly —blessed by the devotion of affluent and generous citizens whose interests were steadily growing in culture and sophistication. The founding and support of cultural institutions appeared to be a way to enrich the city which would be a healthy antidote to the problems that faced the community in the eighties and nineties. It has been noted that Chicagoans toward the end of the century had a way of by-passing New York for Paris, where the agricultural implements and other products they were manufacturing were attracting a healthy international market, and where they became captivated by the art and refinement that were seen as the ingredients of a cultivated affluence. Charles Hutchinson was confident as he contemplated the cultural future of his city: "No lover of art," he wrote, "should be pessimistic regarding Chicago's art future, as in no other city do the citizens show such appreciation of the Art Institute, the park system, and the playgrounds." Already the Art Institute was attracting more than half-a-million people a year, often 3,000 visitors on a Sunday afternoon.

Despite these evidences of confidence and vision, and the hope that the Art Institute would slowly and cautiously acquire original works of art as they became available and as its resources permitted, it was expected that for a long time the galleries would have to be made up of the plaster casts which by 1890 constituted one of the largest such collections in the country. William M. R. French, the Art Institute's first director, thought that the collections could be further developed by adding some inexpensive objects such as reproductions of metal work and ivory autotypes. But Hutchinson and his associates realized that only the acquisition of original masterpieces would build a cultural institution of quality and distinction. Aided by Mr. French, they watched movements in the art world diligently, as did the Trustees and the able and knowledgeable directors in the years to follow. From the beginning they displayed a willingness to purchase works in a range of periods and styles.

In 1894, Mr. Hutchinson, with the aid of Martin Antoine Ryerson, who remains the largest single benefactor of the Art Institute, and several other donors, seized the opportunity to acquire thirteen major works from the collection of Prince Anatole Demidoff, for the most part paintings by the Dutch Masters. The purchase was a milestone, and the paintings which were acquired are considered among the most valued treasures of the Art Institute to this day. Rembrandt's *Young Girl at an Open Half-Door,* Massys's *Man with a Pink,* and Meindert Hobbema's *The Watermill with the Great Red Roof* (which are included in this book) were part of the Demidoff Collection. The acquisition catapulted the Art Institute into the ranks of America's foremost museums.

Within a few years, the collection was further enriched by a gift from Mrs. Henry Field of forty-one paintings of the Barbizon School, including several examples by Millet, which were given in memory of her husband. By 1900, The Antiquarian Society, an ancillary group formed to support the Art Institute, had contributed a number of important items in the decorative arts field. Louis Tiffany expressed the enthusiasm of many of his contemporaries when he visited the young museum on Chicago's lakefront near the turn of the century: "It is the handsomest public gallery in the country."

In 1906 the Trustees voted (after considerable controversy) to purchase what is considered by many to be the most important painting in the Art Institute's collection—El Greco's *The Assumption of the Virgin.* The painting had formed the central part of the high altarpiece of the Church of San Domingo el Antiguo in Toledo, and was the master's first great Spanish commission.

The Art Institute of Chicago, 1882-93

Charles L. Hutchinson

Chicago Interstate Industrial Exhibition Building (formerly on the site of present Art Institute)

Courtesy of Chicago Historical Society

The Art Institute in 1909. Below: The Gallery of Plaster Casts, 1910

Mrs. Potter Palmer

Mary Cassatt had discovered the painting while traveling in Spain with the Horace Havemeyers of New York in 1901. When the Havemeyers found that they could not accommodate the picture in their collection, they entrusted Mary Cassatt and the dealer Durand-Ruel with its disposal in 1906. Mary Cassatt approached the Art Institute, and although the price of $40,000 seemed prohibitive, Mr. Ryerson and Mr. Hutchinson, impressed by Mary Cassatt's enthusiasm for the work, convinced their colleagues to authorize the acquisition with contributions from various Trustees. A gift in 1915 from Mrs. Nancy Atwood Sprague permitted the original donors to be reimbursed.

The bequest received in 1922 from Mrs. Potter Palmer, and subsequent gifts by her sons Potter, Jr., and Honoré, established the Art Institute at once as a foremost repository of French Impressionist painting. Bertha Honoré Palmer's role in the social and cultural life of Chicago was unparalleled. As the chairman of the Board of Lady Managers of the World's Columbian Exposition, she was, as she herself put it, "the nation's hostess." An invitation to the Palmer castle on Lake Shore Drive and its art gallery was highly coveted indeed.

Not content with collecting T'ang figurines, late Chinese porcelains, and other *objets d'art,* Mr. and Mrs. Palmer turned with enthusiasm to contemporary paintings. A visit to Monet in 1891 resulted in the purchase of the first of many of his paintings which the Palmers were to acquire. *The River* is a notable example. It was fortuitous that friendship with Mary Cassatt brought Mrs. Palmer in touch with the group of painters who were challenging the authority of the French Academy with such vigor: Manet, Monet, Pissarro, Degas, Renoir. Soon the Palmers' new picture gallery was graced by many of their works, paintings that were to be a prized and important part of the Art Institute's magnificent Impressionist collection. Among the Impressionist masterpieces chosen for this centennial treasury, several paintings are from the Palmer bequest: Renoir's *Two Little Circus Girls* and *The Rowers' Lunch,* and, as has already been mentioned, *The River* by Claude Monet.

The W. W. Kimball Collection, which was given to the Art Institute in 1922, included three magnificent portraits: Rembrandt's *Portrait of the Artist's Father,* Sir Joshua Reynolds's *Lady Sarah Bunbury Sacrificing to the Graces,* and Sir Thomas Lawrence's *Mrs. Jens Wolff.* Clearly, Chicago collectors had not forsaken the older masters in their enthusiasm for the works of their own day.

The Helen Birch Bartlett Memorial Collection was given to the Art Institute by Frederic Clay Bartlett in memory of his wife. The most notable painting in this group is Seurat's *Sunday Afternoon on the Island of La Grande Jatte,* one of the best-known paintings in the world. Van Gogh's *Bedroom at Arles,* Toulouse-Lautrec's *At the Moulin Rouge,* Cézanne's *The Basket of Apples,* Picasso's *The Old Guitarist,* and Gauguin's *The Day of the God* are further testimony to the quality and range of the Bartlett gift.

Despite the readiness of many Chicago collectors to accept the *avant-garde,* the display of the Armory Show of 1913 at the Art Institute brought a mixed response. Director W.M.R. French was especially cool, remarking privately that the show had in it "a large element of hoax and humbug and another large element of laziness and incompetence." Charles Hutchinson was tolerant but restrained, believing that the many talented and competent artists represented were entitled to experiment. Harriet Monroe, editor of *Poetry* magazine, writing in the Chicago *Sunday Tribune,* pleaded for patience and objectivity. "Either these pictures are good or they are not. If they are good, they will make their way in spite of objections; if they are not, they will perish without the aid of objections." It is not surprising that the public reaction was mixed. The Chicago of 1914 (one year later) is described by Carl Sandburg in his famous poem as the "brawling City of the Big Shoulders," hardly a fertile field for early nonrepresentational art.

The Art Institute, however, is unquestionably richer today for several of the Expressionist works from the 1913 show which later became part of the collection of Arthur Jerome Eddy, a Chicago lawyer, who became greatly interested

The Field Collection of Barbizon Paintings. Below: The Chicago Armory Show, 1913

in the art of the early twentieth century. Eddy, in fact, wrote the first book by an American on modern art and assembled a noteworthy collection, which was bequeathed to the Art Institute in 1931. Kandinsky's *Improvisation with Green Center, No. 176* is a notable example of the works in this group.

The extensive contributions of Mr. and Mrs. Martin A. Ryerson deserve special mention. Their gifts spanned many decades—from the magnificent Rembrandt that joined the Art Institute collection in 1894 to the group of 227 paintings, together with Oriental and decorative arts and textiles, that were left to the Art Institute at Mr. Ryerson's death. The Ryersons' interests were as impeccable as they were wide-ranging. The Art Institute was always on their minds as they traveled in Europe and Asia (often with their good friends the Hutchinsons) in search of new artistic wonders. The multitude of masterpieces that caught Mr. Ryerson's eye is represented in this volume by many diverse works: the fourteenth-century Italian *Crucifixion*; Giovanni di Paolo's *Salome Begs for St. John's Head*, one of the six scenes from the *Life of John the Baptist* owned by the Art Institute; Rogier van der Weyden's *Madonna and Child*; *The Ascension* by the Master of Moulins; Rembrandt's *Young Girl at an Open Half-Door*; Monet's *Old St. Lazare Station, Paris*; Renoir's *Lady at the Piano*; Degas' *Dancers in the Wings*. The Ryerson bequest was not only the most important to come to the Art Institute, but also one of the major gifts to be received by any public institution in the United States.

The Art Institute's distinguished collection of nineteenth-century French painting was further augmented by the gift of Mrs. Lewis Larned Coburn, who died in 1933. The reader will notice that several of the Impressionist masterpieces in this book are from the Coburn collection: Monet, *The Beach at Sainte Adresse*; Degas, *The Millinery Shop*; Cézanne, *Vase of Tulips*.

An immeasurable contribution to the Art Institute's holdings in Japanese and European prints, Chinese ritual bronzes, and medieval art and artifacts was made by the Buckingham family—Kate Sturges, Clarence, and Lucy Maud. Chicagoans had been introduced to Japanese prints when a Japanese Pavilion was included in the World's Columbian Exposition. Clarence Buckingham started buying prints as early as 1894, and he sought every opportunity to strengthen his collection. He was guided by Frederick W. Gookin, an outstanding American authority on Japanese prints and a primary collector. Many of the Buckingham prints, and others from the collections of Gookin, Dr. J. Clarence Webster, John H. Wrenn, and Frank Lloyd Wright, were exhibited in 1908 in a beautiful and epoch-making installation designed by Wright.

After Buckingham's sudden death in 1913, his sister Kate, who had inherited the collection and the family fortune, deposited the prints at the Institute. Two years later, seven hundred prints from the collection were placed on public exhibition in seven large galleries, with a catalogue by Gookin, who had been appointed as Keeper of the Clarence Buckingham Collection of Japanese Prints.

Kate Sturges Buckingham gave impressive examples of early Chinese ceremonial bronzes, early Chinese stone sculptures, and ceramics to the Institute in memory of her sister. She continued until her death to augment the Japanese print collection and bequeathed a major fund to the Institute for the care of the collections and for further acquisitions. Her generosity can also be seen in the beautiful Clarence Buckingham Memorial Fountain in Grant Park, not far from the Art Institute on the lake front, which was given in

Martin A. Ryerson and Claude Monet in the artist's garden

The Ryersons and Hutchinsons in India

Japanese Print exhibit in the Buckingham Gallery, 1908, designed by Frank Lloyd Wright. Below: View of the Central Foyer, 1910

The new interior staircase, soon after its installation. Below: Blackstone Hall

memory of her brother and is administered by the Trustees of the Institute.

A fine collection of Oriental pottery and porcelain assembled by Kate Buckingham and Mr. and Mrs. Potter Palmer, Jr., grew under the patronage of Russell Tyson. For forty years, until his death in 1964, Mr. Tyson selected and gave many very fine examples of Chinese, Korean, and Japanese ceramics to the Institute.

The collection of Charles H. and Mary F. S. Worcester was developed for the express purpose of complementing and strengthening the Art Institute's holdings, and Cecco del Caravaggio's *The Resurrection*, Veronese's *Creation of Eve*, and Millet's *Horse* are worthy examples of their connoisseurship.

In 1921, Joseph Winterbotham set up a trust fund with the provision that the income be spent on modern European pictures, the total to be limited to thirty-five. It was understood that the quality of this group was to be carefully maintained, and administered by a committee. Individual works could be sold, and replacements purchased, if such adjustments seemed warranted—a unique and forward-looking provision. Many of the paintings which are a part of the Joseph Winterbotham Collection are included in this book: *Patience*, by Balthus; *The Rabbi of Vitebsk*, by Chagall; *Inventions of the Monsters*, by Dali; *The Philosopher's Conquest*, by de Chirico; *Woman in a Rose Hat*, by Degas; *Champ de Mars, the Red Tower*, by Delaunay; *Time Transfixed*, by Magritte; *Portrait of a Woman (Juanita Obrador)*, by Miró; and *Self Portrait*, by Van Gogh.

Important gifts to the Art Institute were made in the 1920s by the Deering family. Charles Deering and his brother James acquired many significant examples of fourteenth- and fifteenth-century Spanish works, including *The Ayala Altar*. One of the superb paintings given by James Deering is Tiepolo's *Rinaldo Enchanted by Armida*, which is illustrated in this volume.

The tradition of giving that has been so much a part of Chicago's heritage and such a crucial element in the Institute's legacy from the past is being unquestionably sustained by the present generation of donors and Trustees. Many of the masterpieces in this book have been given by donors who are currently active: *The Crystal Palace*, by Pissarro, given by Mr. and Mrs. B. E. Bensinger; *Portrait of a Man as Don Quixote*, by Fragonard, *Man with a Pipe*, by Picasso, and *Portrait of Picasso*, by Gris, given by Mr. and Mrs. Leigh B. Block; *That Which I Should Have Done I Did Not Do*, by Albright, given by Mr. and Mrs. Leigh B. Block and Mr. Earle Ludgin; *Mother and Child*, by Picasso, given by Mr. and Mrs. Leigh B. Block, Mr. and Mrs. Edwin E. Hokin, Mrs. Maurice L. Rothschild, and others; *The Slave Market*, by de La Hyre, and *Still Life with Monkey, Fruits and Flowers*, by Oudry, from gifts of Mrs. Eugene A. Davidson to the Major Acquisitions Centennial Fund. Also shown are: *Diagonal Composition*, 1921, by Mondrian, and *Excavation*, by de Kooning, given by Mr. Edgar Kaufmann, Jr.; *Portrait of General José Manuel Romero*, by Goya, given by Mr. Charles Deering McCormick; and *Self Portrait*, by Bazille, and *Salome with the Head of John the Baptist*, by Reni, given by Mr. and Mrs. Frank H. Woods.

The generosity of Trustees is evident not only in the collections and in the building but in unrestricted funds and gifts for operating purposes and special needs. In this regard William McCormick Blair, a Life Trustee and President Emeritus, merits special mention.

THE BUILDING

Inevitably the ever-increasing number of objects housed within the Institute's walls and a continuous growth in attendance have required additional space and more and more complex facilities. The building designed by Shepley, Rutan and Coolidge was a fireproof structure of Bedford limestone in the style of an Italian Renaissance palace. The relation to the Renaissance was no mere architectural conceit—it was a reflection of deeply held convictions concerning the nature of art and public buildings. In the nineties—a golden age of cultural improvement and philanthropy—Chicago's citizens drew a comparison between the commercial expansion and artistic flowering of Florence during

Lunch in McKinlock Court. Below: Stanley McCormick Court

Photograph by Hedrich-Blessing

Outdoor figure painting class in McKinlock Court, circa 1937

the Renaissance and their own flourishing business ventures and deepening cultural commitment. Shepley, Rutan and Coolidge, who also designed the Chicago Public Library, in 1893-94, were considered masters in the architecture of monumental and impressive public buildings. Their traditional approach contrasted with the innovative designs of the Chicago architects of the day, Adler, Sullivan, and Root; however, this classical style, dictated by the directors of the Columbian Exposition, meshed well with the public sentiment that demanded an impressive, dignified structure that would symbolize the didactic nature and timelessness of art. The building they designed was both aesthetically commanding and technically efficient. It has stood the test of time well and functions to this very day as a workable exhibition space and a gracious architectural expression of the seriousness of Chicago's commitment to the arts.

The last century has brought many changes and additions to the original building of the Art Institute. The central portion was in time named for Robert Allerton, an early Trustee, Honorary President, and great benefactor over the years, through contributions and generous trust funds. In 1895, Mrs. Henry Field presented the Art Institute with the famous bronze lions designed by Edward L. Kemeys, which stand at the Michigan Avenue entrance. In 1897, Fullerton Hall, a 500-seat auditorium given by Charles W. Fullerton, was put to immediate use with a lecture series on painting, sculpture, and architecture given by the city's most prominent artists.

The Ryerson Library, the gift of Mr. and Mrs. Martin A. Ryerson, was opened in 1901, and remains one of the most valuable research and reference sources for art scholars in the Chicago area. Blackstone Hall, a gift of Mr. and Mrs. Timothy B. Blackstone, was built along the east side of the building next to the Illinois Central Railroad Tracks.

With the completion of Gunsaulus Hall in 1910 the Art Institute actually spanned the adjacent railroad tracks. The main floor of this addition was named for the clergyman Dr. Frank C. Gunsaulus, and was the gift of William H. Miner. It has provided additional exhibition space for the Industrial Arts collection.

The new monumental interior staircase was described in the Annual Report of 1910–11: "Nothing since the original erection of the Art Institute has done so much as the construction of this grand staircase to dignify and ennoble the building. Immediately upon entering the visitor is aware that he is in a great public building devoted to art." This architectural element continues to serve as an impressive gateway to the painting galleries.

In 1920, the Hutchinson Wing, named for Charles L. Hutchinson, was constructed for the Oriental Collection. At the same time Mr. and Mrs. George A. McKinlock gave a garden court in memory of their son, George Alexander McKinlock, Jr., which was at first used in the summer months for sketching classes, and later for outdoor dining. The Swedish American Committee, a group of Americans of Swedish descent, gave *The Fountain of the Tritons* by Carl Milles, a copy of the fountain at Lidingö, Sweden, to adorn the center of a rectangular pool in the McKinlock Court.

The Kenneth Sawyer Goodman Memorial Theatre was built in 1925 by Mr. and Mrs. William O. Goodman in memory of their son, a poet-playwright who died during World War I. In this 683-seat theatre, the first of its kind to be built as part of a museum, three generations of Chicagoans have seen scores of experimental and classical productions. In the future, plays in the Goodman Theatre will be produced by the Chicago Theatre Group, Inc., which was established in September 1977. In 1978, the Goodman Theatre School of Drama became part of DePaul University.

The Alonzo C. Mather addition was constructed in 1926 and the Agnes Allerton Wing in 1927–28. The latter facility has housed textiles, furniture, tapestries, and related arts. Other than landscaping in preparation for the Art Institute's Century of Progress exhibition, the thirties and forties saw little external change in the building, although the collection itself grew rapidly.

In 1958 a major addition, the five-story B. F. Ferguson Memorial Building, which houses the administrative and curatorial offices and the technical services of the Art Institute, was completed. During the same period new Oriental Galleries were opened, the Print and Drawing Galleries were reconstructed, and the Glore Print Study Room, a gift of Mrs. Charles F. Glore in memory of her husband, a Trustee, was created. The Morton Lecture Hall, a gift of Mrs. Sterling Morton, and the Lacy Armour Gallery, a gift of Mrs. Laurance H. Armour, were further additions.

Two courts were given to the Art Institute by Mrs. Stanley McCormick in memory of her husband: the north court (1960) in front of the Ferguson Building at Michigan Avenue and Monroe Street, and the south court (1966) in front of the Morton Wing. In 1960, the Thorne Rooms were installed in their present location. These sixty-seven miniature rooms, a gift of their creator, Mrs. James Ward Thorne, serve as a popular attraction to both the casual observer and the student of period furnishings.

The School of the Art Institute moved into new quarters east of the Illinois Central Railroad tracks in 1961. In 1962, the Morton Wing, which added valuable space for exhibition and storage, was given by Sterling and Preston O. Morton. The three-story building, located to the south of the Allerton Building, houses the permanent collection of nineteenth- and twentieth-century European painting and sculpture and provides space for special exhibitions. Both the Ferguson Building on the north and the Morton Wing on the south are constructed of Bedford limestone to match the central 1893 façade. The structures differ from the original building in the simplicity of their design.

The Junior Museum, a joint project of the Woman's Board of the Art Institute and the Junior League of Chicago, was opened on February 13, 1964, in the Michigan Avenue building.

The year 1968 saw the opening of the A. Montgomery Ward Gallery and the relocation of the Burnham Library of Architecture, a semi-circular ambulatory on the floor above the main reading room of the Ryerson Library.

Through the generosity of Mrs. Joseph Regenstein, the study rooms and galleries for Prints and Drawings were rehabilitated and reconstructed in 1972. The estate of Margaret Day Blake also contributed substantially to this reconstruction. Both of these donors have considerably augmented the Institute's collections of outstanding master drawings.

The Art Institute today, as seen from the east against the Chicago skyline

Photograph by Hedrich-Blessing

The Centennial Fund

In 1972, under President Leigh B. Block, the Art Institute inaugurated the Centennial Fund, a master plan to raise $46.4 million for improvement and expansion, which was to culminate in the Centennial observance of 1979. The Centennial Fund campaign was chaired by Trustee Charles C. Haffner III. Planning had begun almost a decade earlier, when the Trustees and staff realized that the existing facility did not adequately accommodate the institution's needs. The collections were growing, and the curators were becomingly increasingly concerned about security problems and the lack of adequate climate controls. The School of the Art Institute had long since outgrown its quarters and was renting inadequate downtown office space for additional classroom use. It became clear that these and other difficulties could only be solved through a major construction program.

The firm of Skidmore, Owings & Merrill was retained, and work on architectural land-use studies began in earnest. The final master plan reflects projected growth trends and anticipated needs for the next quarter-century. The building which resulted is the beautiful Columbus Drive addition designed by Walter A. Netsch, which won a 1978 national American Institute of Architects award.

The Centennial Fund has provided for the following basic expansions of the Art Institute's plant through a program initiated in May 1974:

A new facility has been developed to house the studios, classrooms, and laboratories of the School, including a students' gallery, an auditorium for films and lectures, and other facilities. The building added about 133,000 square feet of space on four levels, including special areas for film, television, design, sculpture, ceramics, a library, printmaking, photography, weaving, drawing, painting, and administration.

The McKinlock Court Galleries have added about 17,000 square feet of new exhibition space by the construction of a second level around the court. The Primitive Art collection and parts of the large Twentieth Century Painting and Sculpture collection are displayed here.

The Trading Room from the Chicago Stock Exchange Building was reconstructed on the first floor in the new Columbus Drive facilities through a generous grant from the Walter E. Heller Foundation and its president, Mrs. Edwin J. DeCosta. The architectural elements from this renowned Chicago landmark were given by the City of Chicago, Mrs. Eugene A. Davidson, The Graham Foundation, and the Three Oaks Wrecking Company. The Entrance Arch from the Chicago Stock Exchange Building was given by the City of Chicago and reconstructed in the new east gardens near Monroe Drive by the Walter E. Heller Foundation.

New dining facilities have been constructed next to McKinlock Court.

A new 950-seat auditorium, equipped with up-to-date film and sound equipment, has been located adjacent to the new Columbus Drive entrance, so that programs and seminars can be scheduled for evening hours without compromising the security of the galleries.

The Columbus Drive entrance has provided easy, safe access to the Institute for school buses and motorists, as well as for the handicapped.

The Centennial Fund has also supplied resources for the strengthening of the Art Institute's existing resources. Additional endowment has helped to provide income for operating support as well as a special revolving major acquisitions fund. Contributions from the Centennial Fund have also assisted in the revision of exhibition space for all departments. New fire-detection equipment and a new security system have been installed. New air-conditioning and environmental-control equipment has been purchased, and improved conservation and storage facilities for the protection of the collection have been provided.

The major funds for this drive were contributed by the Chicago Park District; Trustees, corporations, foundations, and the citizens of Chicago.

Two artistic additions made to the building in the early seventies are especially noteworthy.

On November 30, 1976, a fountain sculpture by Isamu Noguchi, commissioned by the Trus-

Photograph by Hedrich-Blessing

Sculpture by Isamu Noguchi

Photograph © by Howard N. Kaplan

The Entrance Arch and the Trading Room from the Chicago Stock Exchange Building by Adler and Sullivan

tees of the B. F. Ferguson Monument Fund, was dedicated. The sculpture, celebrating the 200th Anniversary of the Founding of the Republic, is placed in a reflecting pool adjacent to the new Columbus Drive entrance. The B. F. Ferguson Monument Fund, administered by the Trustees of The Art Institute of Chicago, has been used for the erection and maintenance of statuary and monuments in many parks and public places.

The *America Windows*, created by Marc Chagall as a memorial to Chicago's late Mayor Richard J. Daley, and commemorating the Bicentennial, were dedicated on May 15, 1977. The six monumental stained-glass windows were given by the City of Chicago and the Auxiliary Board of the Art Institute and are installed in the Marc Chagall Gallery, also a gift from this Board. They are the only Chagall windows in an American museum.

THE AUXILIARY SOCIETIES

Our brief history here has barely touched on the debt that is owed by the Art Institute and the community it serves to its many thousands of members and the scores of citizens who have given time, energy, and financial resources to the development and maintenance of its collections. The role of the ancillary societies which have served the Art Institute so well for so much of the century, and continue to do so, deserves special recognition.

The scope of the contributions made to the Art Institute by The Antiquarian Society, the oldest of the auxiliary groups, was evident in a major exhibition of 1977—"The Antiquarian Society of The Art Institute of Chicago: The First One Hundred Years"—in which 600 works given to the Institute by the Society were displayed. The Antiquarian Society has had a distinguished record of accomplishment. Early collecting was in the field of textiles, but the Society has broadened its range to include all of the decorative arts, and has presented major gifts in American Arts, Earlier Painting and Sculpture, European Decorative Arts, Primitive Art, and Prints and Drawings. The purchases, exhibitions, and lectures of The Antiquarian Society have made a contribution to the first century of the Art Institute that cannot be overstated.

The Print and Drawing Club, founded in 1922, has brought the richness and depth of the Institute's magnificent collection to an enthusiastic and devoted membership. At regular meetings the curatorial staff has led lecture-discussions on works from the collection. Funds contributed by the club have enabled the Print and Drawing Department to purchase a number of significant and important works.

Founded in 1925 by a group of collectors, The Orientals has maintained a tradition of notable gifts to the Art Institute and a devotion to scholarship. The society's first gifts were a Persian Gabri bowl of the ninth to tenth century A.D. and a Chinese Ting Yao ceramic bowl of the Sung dynasty with molded decorations of bamboo and morning glory.

The knowledge and taste of the members of the Society for Contemporary Art are reflected in the superb gifts made to the Institute's contemporary collection. A few examples are: Jules Olitski, *Green Marfak*; Joseph Raffael, *Water Painting IX*; Bridget Riley, *Ascending and Descending Hero*; Ben Shahn, *Mine Disaster*; Alexander Calder, *3 x 5 Plus 1*; Adolph Gottlieb, *Expanding*; and Jackson Pollock, *Grayed Rainbow*, which is reproduced in this book.

Since its founding in 1894, the Chicago Public School Art Society has provided enrichment to generations of Chicago schoolchildren through art reproductions, lectures, and programs. The Society became affiliated with the Art Institute in 1946 and has given continuous and generous scholarship assistance to the School.

The Woman's Board was established in 1952. Five standing committees form the backbone of the Board. The Community Associates manages twelve affiliate groups—eleven suburban, one urban—totaling about 5,000 women, all of whom are Art Institute members. The Art Rental and Sales Committee operates the gallery for the works of approximately 300 local artists. The Junior Museum Committee, assisted by the Junior League of Chicago, organized the volunteer Staff Assistant program, planned and

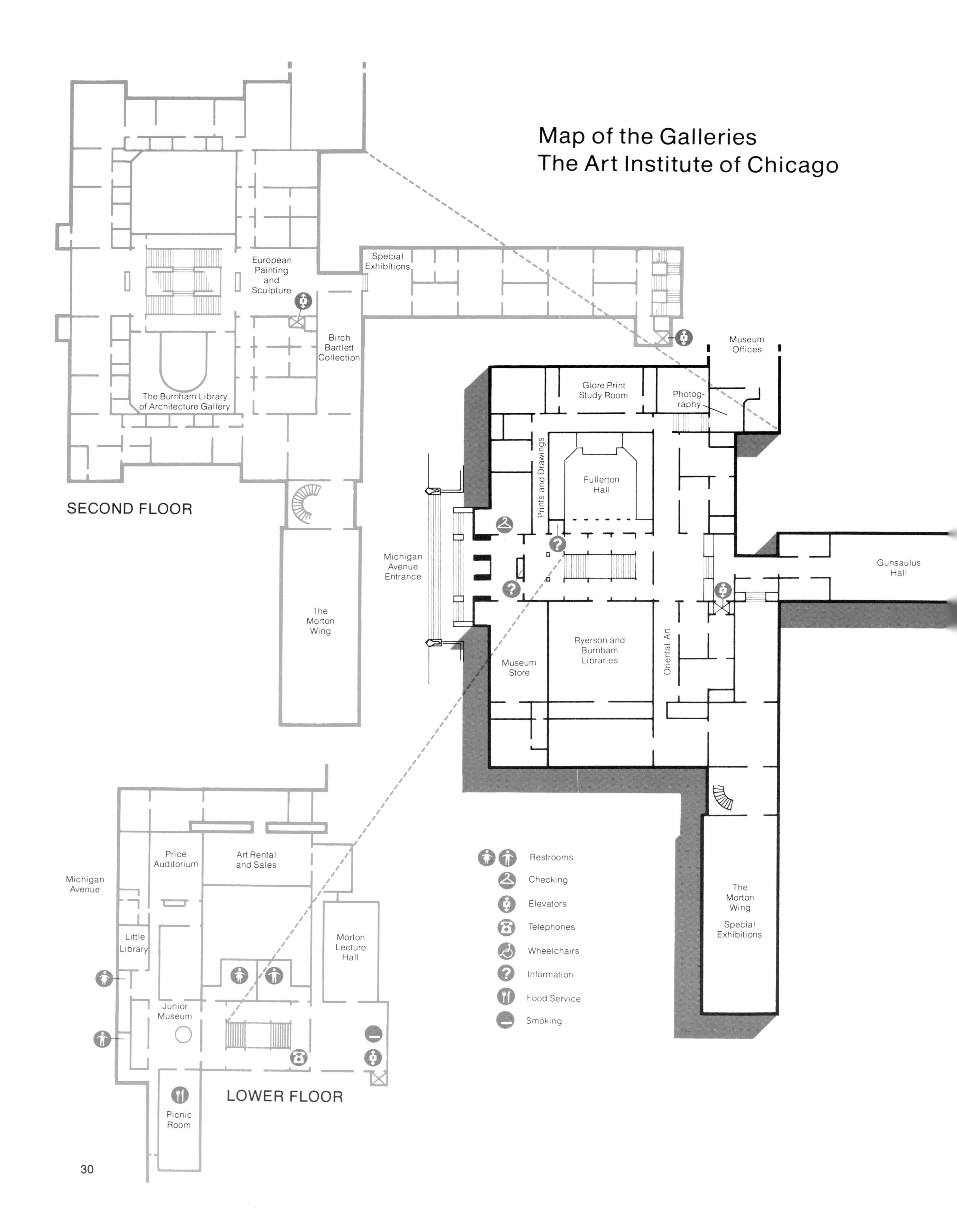
Map of the Galleries
The Art Institute of Chicago
SECOND FLOOR
European Painting and Sculpture
Special Exhibitions
Birch Bartlett Collection
The Burnham Library of Architecture Gallery
The Morton Wing
Museum Offices
Glore Print Study Room
Photog-raphy
Prints and Drawings
Fullerton Hall
Michigan Avenue Entrance
Gunsaulus Hall
Museum Store
Ryerson and Burnham Libraries
Oriental Art
The Morton Wing
Special Exhibitions
Restrooms
Checking
Elevators
Telephones
Wheelchairs
Information
Food Service
Smoking
Michigan Avenue
Price Auditorium
Art Rental and Sales
Little Library
Morton Lecture Hall
Junior Museum
LOWER FLOOR
Picnic Room

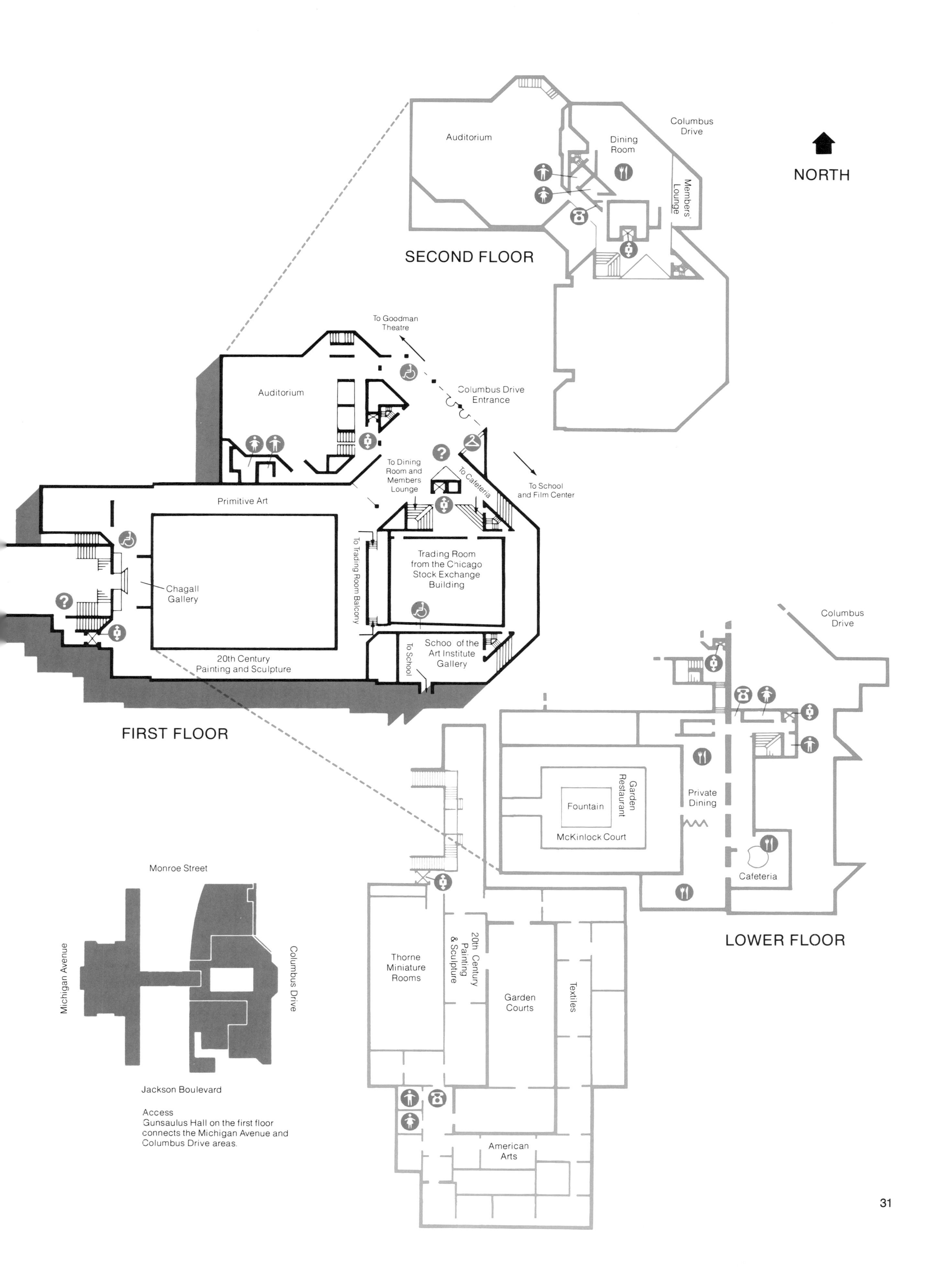

NORTH
SECOND FLOOR
Auditorium
Dining Room
Columbus Drive
Members' Lounge
FIRST FLOOR
To Goodman Theatre
Auditorium
Columbus Drive Entrance
To Dining Room and Members Lounge
To Cafeteria
To School and Film Center
Primitive Art
Chagall Gallery
To Trading Room Balcony
Trading Room from the Chicago Stock Exchange Building
School of the Art Institute Gallery
To School
20th Century Painting and Sculpture
LOWER FLOOR
Columbus Drive
Garden Restaurant
Fountain
McKinlock Court
Private Dining
Cafeteria
Thorne Miniature Rooms
20th Century Painting & Sculpture
Garden Courts
Textiles
American Arts
Monroe Street
Michigan Avenue
Columbus Drive
Jackson Boulevard
Access
Gunsaulus Hall on the first floor connects the Michigan Avenue and Columbus Drive areas.

funded the construction of the Junior Museum, and continues to contribute generously to its promotion and support. The Hospitality Committee concerns itself with many levels of entertaining, from large functions welcoming new members to receptions for delegations from other museums around the country. The youngest committee, the Volunteer Committee, three years old, has been responsible for coordinating the efforts of a group of energetic and dedicated volunteers who give some 1,500 hours per month to tasks ranging from filing to research.

Since its founding in 1972 the Auxiliary Board has worked with energy and dedication to support the Art Institute in many innovative and creative ways, including the Marc Chagall project, "Sculpture in the Park," an exhibition of contemporary sculpture shown in Grant Park near the Art Institute; "Art in the Park," which provided art and dance instruction for city children and adults in selected Chicago parks; and "Music for the Collections," a series of free concerts at the Art Institute.

The Old Masters Society was founded in 1977 as an adjunct to the Department of Earlier Painting. It is expected to provide welcome support in an area that had not previously been served by an Institute affiliate.

The Textile Society, which is in formation, aims to further the appreciation of textiles, encourage private collections, provide lectures and programs, contribute funds for special publications and exhibitions, and supplement the acquisition funds of the department.

The Sustaining Fellows of The Art Institute of Chicago was initiated by the Board of Trustees to honor individuals and corporations providing significant annual support. The contributions of the Sustaining Fellows will be directed toward an area of critical need—current operating expenses.

THE ART INSTITUTE TODAY

Through the century The Art Institute of Chicago has evolved into a complex institution which administers many diverse activities in the fields of education and fine arts.

The School of the Art Institute

The School of the Art Institute is the leading institution for the training of the artist in the United States and the only major degree granting art school that has remained connected with a major museum—an affiliation that provides a superb laboratory of models in every media.

The new Columbus Drive building adds greatly improved facilities to an outstanding faculty and a broadly based curriculum that grants both undergraduate and graduate degrees, and includes painting, sculpture, printmaking, film-making, video art, photography, fashion design, ceramics, and fiber and fabric, as well as courses in art history, art education, and the liberal arts.

The contributions of the School's alumni to the artistic life of their times testify to the quality and vitality of the academic program. Several are represented in this book. Georgia O'Keeffe, Ivan Albright, and Grant Wood. Claes Oldenburg, Richard Hunt, Thomas Hart Benton, Richard Lippold, Theodore Roszak, and Halston are among the many alumni who have achieved distinction.

The Film Center administered by the School has entered its fifth year of expanded programming and community services, fully supported by grants, subscriptions, and ticket sales. The best in classic and contemporary cinema is presented, whether European or American, fact or fiction, historical or *avant garde*. The public programs presented four evenings a week, for forty-four weeks of the year, have attracted thousands of Chicagoans.

The Department of Earlier Painting

The importance of the Department of Earlier Painting has been demonstrated, of course, by the many paintings that have been chosen for this book. A number of major exhibitions have been organized by this department during the century. The following are especially noteworthy: the Century of Progress exhibitions in 1933 and 1934; Goya, 1941; the Hudson River School, 1945; Cézanne, 1952 and 1971; Whistler, Sargent, and Mary Cassatt, 1954; Toulouse-Lautrec, 1956; Seurat, 1958; Manet, 1966; Renoir, 1973; Monet, 1974; Bazille, 1978. Many of the department's exhibitions over the years have broken public attendance records.

The Department of Twentieth Century Painting and Sculpture

Chicago collectors have always been interested in works by artists of their own time, and the department reflects that interest. The collection is continually expanding, in the effort to acquire significant works from the immediate past and those from present-day artists who give promise of enduring interest.

The Department of Prints and Drawings

Although the collection was begun in 1887 with a gift of a large number of miscellaneous items, it was organized as a separate department in 1911 with Kenneth Sawyer Goodman as curator. For students and visitors who wish to experience works of special intimacy and sophistication, the Art Institute's superb collections of drawings, watercolors, and sketchbooks are a rich resource.

The Department of Photography

Originally incorporated in the Department of Prints and Drawings, the Photography Department was organized separately in 1959, when an active program of exhibitions and collections was begun. A collection of superlative quality has been formed, and its development is one of the priorities of the next decades.

The Department of Oriental Art

The Department of Oriental Art was established in 1924 when the size and importance of the collection made it impractical to continue it as a part of the Decorative Arts Department. Chicago was famous in the early twentieth century for important collections of Japanese woodblock prints, Chinese porcelains, and archaic Chinese bronzes, many of which were given to the Museum. More recently, Japanese screens and sculpture, Indian sculpture, and Persian and Indian miniature paintings have joined these earlier distinguished gifts.

The Department of European Decorative Arts

The acquiring of decorative arts began in 1896 with the help of The Antiquarian Society. Although the collection originally consisted largely of textiles, Medieval and Renaissance objects were added in the years between the turn of the century and World War I. The department itself was organized in 1921. In recent years it has acquired major eighteenth-century Italian and French pieces of special interest.

The Department of American Arts

The Department of American Arts was founded in 1975. Collections administered by the department include architecture and decorative arts from the seventeenth century to the present, and painting and sculpture from the seventeenth century to 1901.

The Department of Primitive Art

The Department of Primitive Art, which was founded in the 1950s, is one of the centers of ethnographic art in the Midwest. It is a well-developed collection with a very good representation of the highest aesthetic examples of the art of Africa, Oceania, and Native America —North and South. Its ancient Peruvian holdings are among the best in the world.

The Department of Classical Art

As early as the turn of the century the Art Institute housed important examples of classical art, notably Greek vases, and classical coins. Rare, ancient glass and jewelry, and stone sculpture were added in the next few decades. Not until 1974 was an advisory committee formed and the department established as a separate division.

The Department of Textiles

The Department of Textiles developed from the Antiquarian Society's gift of a number of vestments and tapestries in the 1890s into the most comprehensive collection of Western textiles in the Midwest. Now organized as an independent entity, the Department has recently undergone extensive renovation, which has provided additional space and a superb conservation laboratory.

The Ryerson Reading Room of the Ryerson and Burnham Libraries

The Ryerson and Burnham Libraries

The Ryerson Library, a gift of Mr. and Mrs. Martin A. Ryerson, was founded in 1901, and is one of the major art research libraries in the United States. Its collection includes 128,000 volumes, plus 52,000 exhibition catalogues, a large collection of slides and photographs, and issues of all major art periodicals. One of the Library's special strengths is the architecture collection. The Burnham Library of Architecture, founded in 1912, includes over 20,000 volumes, architectural plans, letters, diaries, reports, photographs, and 11,000 architectural drawings and details of major representatives of the Chicago School of Architecture. The Libraries serve the large curatorial and educational staffs of the Art Institute, providing resources for research on the many objects acquired, and for the preparation of exhibition catalogues and lectures. The Libraries are extensively used by the academic and architectural communities.

The Department of Conservation

The Department of Conservation provides essential services for all departments of the Institute, and its efforts are of course fundamental to the preservation of the collections. Not the least of the department's activities is its constant dedication to the discovery of new and improved methods of conservation, from the most ancient objects to recent modern works.

In this introduction we have tried to give a kaleidoscopic view of the Art Institute's eventful 100-year history and to show its profile as it stands on the threshold of a new century. The Art Institute of Chicago has been graced by the tireless efforts of thousands of Chicago's citizens. Contributors, Trustees, staff, volunteers, members —a community of actors in the cultural drama of a great city. In a sense, a museum provides the opportunity for an on-going, eternal dialogue between great works of art and those who experience them. It is hoped that the masterpieces presented here will suggest the scope and beauty of the treasures which The Art Institute of Chicago has acquired over the last century and will be a link with the paintings and viewers which will be part of this dialogue in the years to come.

The Art Institute of Chicago

100 MASTERPIECES

1

1 Italian, unknown artist,
fourteenth century

Crucifixion, probably 1390–1415
Tempera on panel. 20 x 9¼ in (50.9 x 23.5 cm)
Mr. and Mrs. Martin A. Ryerson Collection
1933.1032

This wonderful panel, in fine condition with its gilding brilliant, its egg-tempera paint unrubbed, and its back painted to imitate porphyry exactly, was a devotional object known as a pax. Surprisingly, specialists do not agree on the artist or even the date, but there is some convincing evidence that the panel should be attributed to Don Lorenzo Monaco. It does seem reasonably sure, however, that the artist was a Florentine.

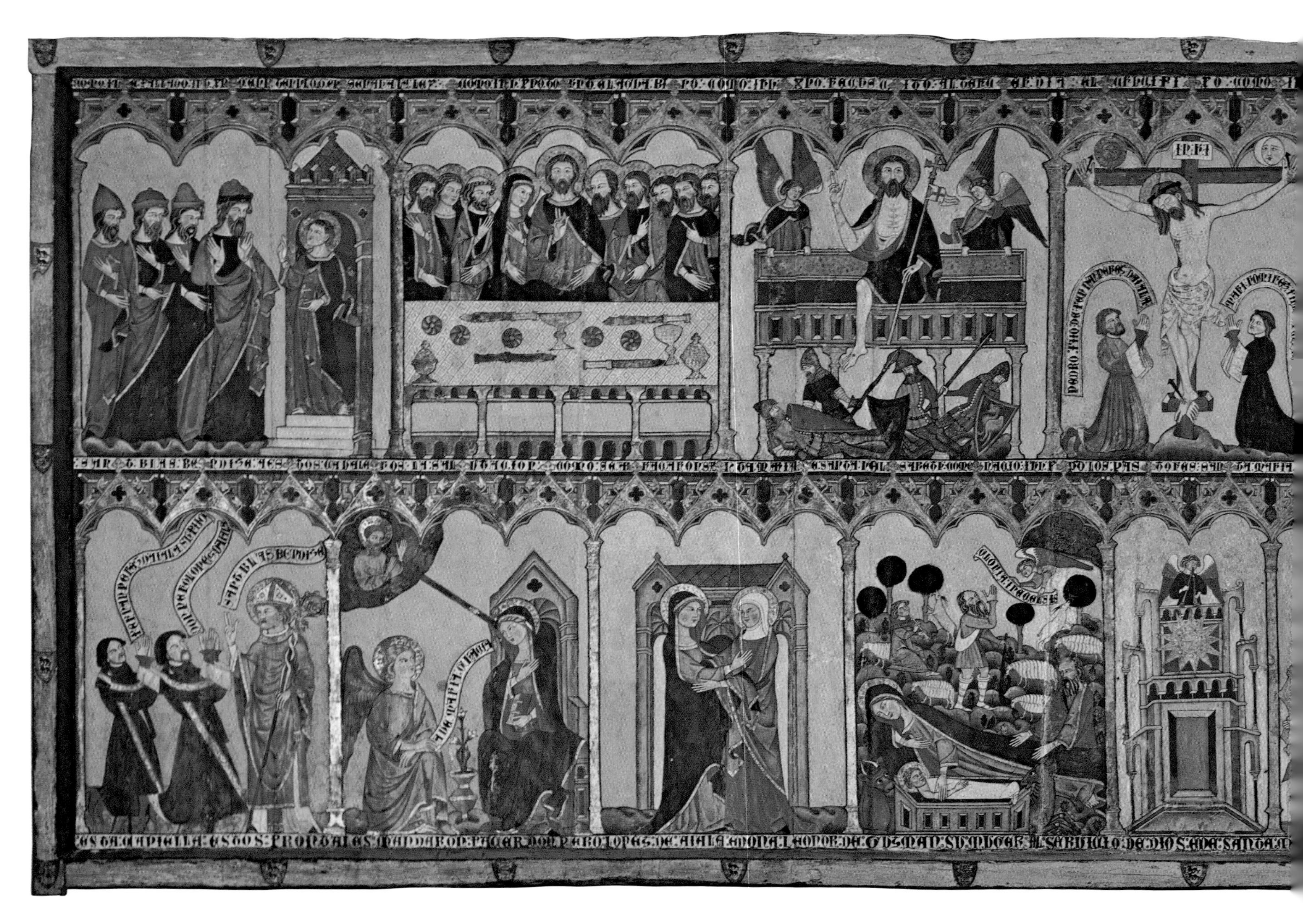

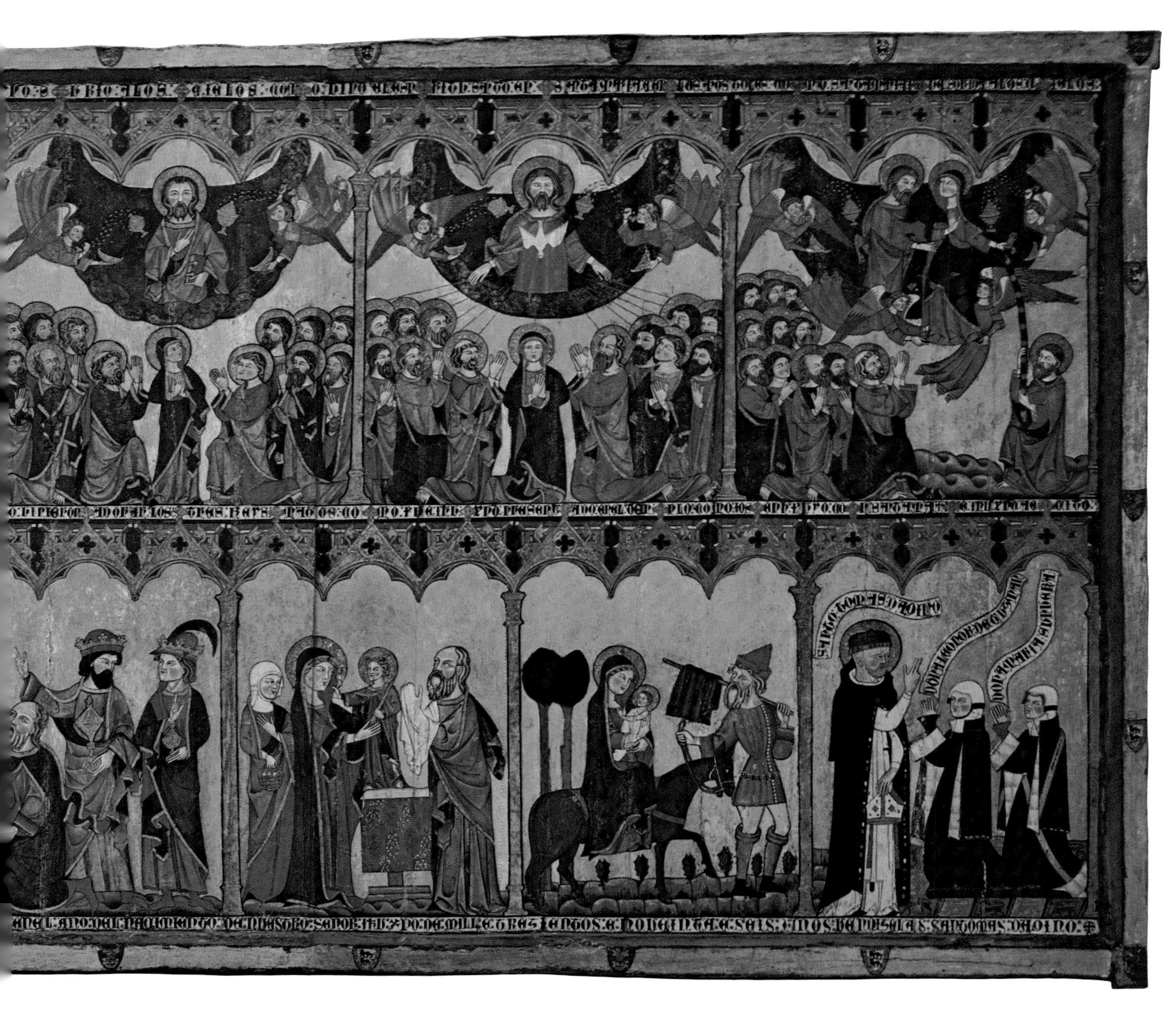

[2] Spanish, unknown artist, *fourteenth century*

The Ayala Altar, 1396
Tempera on panel. Altarpiece 99¾ x 251¾ in (253.6 x 639.4 cm);
Antependium 33½ x 102 in (85.2 x 259.2 cm)
Gift of Charles Deering 1928.817

This Spanish Medieval painting was ordered by the Chancellor of Castile, Don Pedro Lopez de Ayala, for the funeral chapel of the family convent at Quejana, Ayala, where it remained until Mr. Deering bought it in 1913. The influence of manuscript painting is visible in both the use of the funereal white background and the rendering of the figures and landscape. The narratives are presented, scene by scene, with a straightforward directness.

3

3 Bernardo Martorell,
active 1427–1452 Catalan

St. George and the Dragon, c. 1438
Tempera on panel. 56 x 38 in (142.3 x 96.5 cm)
Gift of Mrs. Richard E. Danielson and
Mrs. Chauncey McCormick 1933.786

Martorell was the principal painter in Catalonia in the second quarter of the fifteenth century. This center panel of an altarpiece, with its strong Flemish influence, reflects Spain's strong connections with Flanders and northern Europe during this period. At first glance the picture looks like a page from a late Gothic manuscript. The figures are depicted in sizes relative to their importance for the narrative, with St. George as the dominant figure in the composition.

4 Giovanni di Paolo,
c.1403–1482/3 Italian

Life of John the Baptist:
Salome Begs for St. John's Head,
c. 1450 or 1460
Tempera on panel. 27 x 14¼ in (68.7 x 36.3 cm)
Mr. and Mrs. Martin A. Ryerson Collection
1913.1013

This brilliant panel is part of a large and famous reredos (the architectural backing behind and above an altar). It shows brilliantly the surviving Gothic touches of Giovanni's style, combined with his personal and rather innocent version of the new wave of the Renaissance that was sweeping Italy in his time. Giovanni's painting shows that contemporary Siena was given to elegance and luxury.

4

5

5 Rogier van der Weyden, *1399/1400–1464* *Flemish*

Madonna and Child, between 1450 and 1460
Oil on panel. 15⅛ x 11⅛ in (38.5 x 28.3 cm)
Mr. and Mrs. Martin A. Ryerson Collection 1933.1052

Because of his masterly craftsmanship and his independence and genius as an innovator and inventor of emotional symbols, Rogier is often considered the most influential painter of the north in the fifteenth century—in the generation just after Jan van Eyck. In this panel one sees his remarkable power of detailed observation and his feeling for grace and poignancy.

6 Sandro Botticelli, *1444/5–1510* (*attributed to*) *Italian*

Madonna and Child with Angels, c. 1470
Oil on panel. D. 13⅛ in (33.4 cm)
Max and Leola Epstein Collection 1954.282

This *tondo* has been identified with that mentioned in the second edition of Vasari as the property of the Prior of San Lorenzo and an example of the master's best work. In spite of its age, the nobility of the concept and the skillfulness of the lines and forms survive. Two hands seem to have worked on the panel. The almost heraldic angels epitomize Botticelli's gracefulness, yet the Virgin and Child have a Florentine form and solidity.

6

7

7 Master of Amiens School,
late fifteenth century French

The Ascension, c. 1480
Oil on panel. 48⅛ x 20 in (117.2 x 50.9 cm)
Mr. and Mrs. Martin A. Ryerson Collection
1933.1057

Amiens is in the north of France, close to Flanders, and the style of this Master is an amalgam of French and Flemish influences. This panel was part of a large carved and gilt altarpiece made for the Charterhouse of Thuison, near Abbeville. The altarpiece was dismantled in 1795, and in 1860 the wing panels were split in order to show both sides.

8 Hans Memling, *c. 1433–94 Flemish*

Madonna and Child, c. 1485
Oil and tempera on panel.
13¾ x 10⅝ in (35.0 x 27.0 cm)
Mr. and Mrs. Martin A. Ryerson Collection
1933.1050

This panel with its matching panel of the donor is a sensitive example of the third generation of fifteenth-century Flemish painting. Memling seems to take van der Weyden's elegance and humanize it. The back of this panel is painted to look like tortoise shell, while its mate has an angel painted into a niche to resemble sculpture. The painting is a devotional object of great luxury.

8

9 Master of Moulins, *active c. 1500* *French*

The Annunciation
Oil on panel, 29 x 20 in (73.7 x 50.9 cm)
Mr. and Mrs. Martin A. Ryerson Collection 1933.1062

This slightly mysterious Master from the Loire valley was strongly under the influence of Hugo van der Goes. The mate to this panel, at the National Gallery in London, represents the *Meeting at the Golden Gate;* the center part is as yet unidentified. The style is already that of the Renaissance, while the influence of the Middle Ages has all but vanished. The Master's imagery of feminine beauty is persuasively lovely.

10 Correggio (Antonio Allegri), *c. 1489–1534* *Italian*

Madonna, Child and St. John the Baptist, 1513–15
Oil on panel. 25¼ x 19¾ in (64.2 x 50.4 cm)
Clyde M. Carr Fund 1965.688

This lovely panel, in a dazzling state of preservation with all the greens intact, shows the earlier style of one of the most enigmatic of High Renaissance Italian painters. Here one even sees reminiscences of German printmakers of the epoch, as well as the obvious influence of Leonardo in the Virgin's face. Yet Correggio's subjects, though idealized, present not the unearthly beauty of Leonardo but a sensuousness that is very much of this earth.

11

12

11 Quentin Massys, *1465/66–1530* *Flemish*

Man with a Pink, 1510–1520
Oil on panel. 17¼ x 11½ in (43.9 x 29.2 cm)
Gift of John J. Glessner 1894.1025

Little is known of Massys's life. Records show that he worked in Antwerp after 1491, and *Man with a Pink* was apparently painted during this period. He was clearly influenced by Leonardo, particularly by his drawings. This is one of the earliest pictures in the group from the Demidoff Collection which Charles L. Hutchinson persuaded his friends to buy for the Art Institute. It was the acquisition of this group which moved the Museum from its status as a minor gallery into a role of distinction.

12 Paolo Veronese, *1528–88* *Italian*

Creation of Eve, c. 1570
Oil on canvas. 31⅞ x 40¼ in (81.0 x 102.2 cm)
Charles H. and Mary F. S. Worcester Collection 1930.286

Veronese was one of the most brilliant Venetian Renaissance painters and the leading decorative painter of his age. This beautiful, rather small work shows the excellence of his coloration and his tender, though factual, attitude toward nature. The creation of Eve is an uncommon subject in paintings—Veronese seems to be responding to the new spirit of the century which was seeking to replace traditional Medieval themes.

13

14

13 El Greco (Domenico Theotocopuli), *1541–1614 Spanish*

The Assumption of the Virgin, 1577
Oil on canvas. 158 x 90 in (401.4 x 228.7 cm)
Gift of Nancy Atwood Sprague in memory of Albert Arnold Sprague 1906.99

This great canvas, one of the most famous pictures in the Art Institute, is the center section of the enormous altarpiece for the high altar of Santo Domingo el Antiguo, Toledo, and was El Greco's first Spanish commission. Although he was thinking of Titian's version of the same subject done for the Frari Church, Venice, fifty years earlier, El Greco has turned a High Renaissance picture into one of the greatest of Mannerist paintings.

14 Cecco del Caravaggio, *active first quarter seventeenth century Italian*

The Resurrection, c. 1600
Oil on canvas. 133½ x 78½ in (339.1 x 199.5 cm)
Charles H. and Mary F. S. Worcester Collection 1934.390

The identification of the artist was Roberto Longhi's, though other scholars attributed the painting to a Fleming, Finson. The actual identity of the artist is of relative unimportance, for the picture is a magnificent evocation of Caravaggio's style, without, to be sure, his intense personal passion and awareness of brutal natural phenomena.

15 Peter Paul Rubens, *1577–1640 Flemish*

Holy Family with Infant St. John and St. Elizabeth, c. 1615
Oil on cradled panel (metal struts). 46 x 35½ in (116.9 x 90.2 cm)
Major Acquisitions Fund 1967.229

Rubens, that most prolific and varied of old masters, has here contemplated the contrasts between age, youth, and types of infancy. In a very shallow space, and with a limited palette, the artist has created a sensitive painting with great charm and brilliance of color. An impression of monumentality is achieved by the way in which the action fills the canvas.

16 Hendrik Terbrugghen, *1588–1629 Dutch*

Denial of St. Peter
Oil on canvas. 51⅝ x 69⅝ in (131.1 x 176.9 cm)
Charles H. and Mary F. S. Worcester Collection 1969.3

Terbrugghen was the finest of the northern followers of Caravaggio. He was the first painter of the Utrecht school to travel to Rome and the only one to be there during Caravaggio's lifetime. Yet his work sounded an intensely personal note. Here there is infinite pathos represented in the remote figure of Jesus, whereas Caravaggio would very likely have relied on gesture to tell his story.

Unknown sculptor, *Flanders c. 1650*
Corpus; boxwood, carved
Gift of the Antiquarian Society 1917.12

16

[17] Guido Reni, *1575–1642 Italian*

Salome with the Head of John the Baptist, c. 1638
Oil on canvas. 97¾ x 68 in (248.5 x 173.0 cm)
Frank H. and Louise B. Woods Purchase Fund 1960.3

This late work by Guido shows him at his most attractive. The fact that the painting is in part unfinished merely adds to its interest in a way that anticipates certain of the "neoclassical" canvases of Picasso. Here Guido transforms the naturalism he had learned from his great Bolognese elders, the Caracci, into a grand and noble style. It is this intensity of expression that led Stendhal to describe him as an "absolutely Mozartian sensibility."

[18] Guercino (G. F. Barbieri), *1591–1666 Italian*

Entombment of Christ, probably 1656
Oil on canvas. 47¾ x 87 in (121.3 x 211.6 cm)
Wilson L. Mead Fund 1956.128

Following the death of Guido Reni, Guercino established himself in Bologna as the leader of the Bolognese school. His work shows Baroque predilections—strong chiaroscuro, warm colors, and sweeping compositional movement. Like the Guido Reni *Salome,* this picture also belonged to the Princes Colonna before the end of the eighteenth century, and as a result of the upheaval during the Napoleonic period, it was eventually taken to England.

Guercino
Martyrdom of St. Bartholomew
Pen and brown ink with brown wash
Gift of Mr. and Mrs. Norman H. Pritchard 1960.832

18

[19] Laurent de La Hyre, *1601–56* *French*

The Slave Market, c. 1639–40
Oil on canvas. 56¾ x 41 in (114 x 104.2 cm)
Major Acquisitions Centennial Fund 1976.292

La Hyre belonged to the second generation of French masters in the classical style. He is notable for his splendid color and the severe stylization of his forms. In addition to painting numerous portraits he etched about forty plates on religious, mythological, and landscape subjects.

[20] Nicolas Poussin, *1594–1665* *French*

St. John on Patmos, between 1645 and 1650
Oil on canvas. 40 x 53½ in (101.7 x 135.9 cm)
A. A. Munger Collection 1930.500

Poussin, who has seemed to be one of the most unapproachable of French painters, has here presented a noble and engaging Roman landscape. St. John is conceived as a Roman river god and is in fact derived from a statue of such a figure. The artist has painted his own Roman campagna with uncommon tenderness.

21

Rembrandt van Rijn
Study of a Female Nude
Pen and brown ink and brown wash
The Margaret Day Blake Collection
1947.464

21 Frans Hals, *1580/85–1666 Dutch*

Portrait of a Lady, 1644
Oil on canvas. 34¼ x 26⅜ in (87 x 67 cm)
Max and Leola Epstein Collection 1954.287

Hals, even at his most dashing moments, is never sentimental and never gives the feeling of overt flattery. One feels here that the subject was plain of face, and Hals shows no reluctance in thus showing her to us. Hals's technique and brushwork exercised an influence far into the nineteenth century, especially on Manet and the Impressionists.

22 Rembrandt van Rijn, *1606–69 Dutch*

Young Girl at an Open Half-Door, 1645
Oil on canvas. 40⅛ x 33⅛ in (102.0 x 84.2 cm)
Mr. and Mrs. Martin A. Ryerson Collection 1894.1022

This painting shows the breadth of the painter's mature style and fully anticipates the austere and monumental forms of his late years. The subject, who wears the uniform of the Amsterdam City Orphanage, probably was not Hendrickje Stoffels, his second wife, whose face haunts most of the master's later pictures of women. The work is reminiscent of the half-length females of Titian which Rembrandt undoubtedly knew through engravings—an evocation of the Venetian past.

23 Jacob van Ruisdael,
1628/9–1682 Dutch

Ruins of Egmond, 1650–60
Oil on canvas. 38⅞ x 51⅛ in (98.9 x 129.9 cm)
Potter Palmer Collection Fund 1947.475

This is one of Ruisdael's noble evocations of nature—poetic and full of love for the effects of scenery, light, and the play of shadows from the clouds. The painting shows the influence of Rembrandt's landscape style as well as of the paintings of Berchem and other Dutch landscape painters.

24

25

24 Sébastien Bourdon, *1616–71* *French*

Presumed Portrait of the Baron de Vauvert, c. 1652–54
Oil on canvas. 41 x 34⅝ in (103.8 x 88.1 cm)
Charles H. and Mary F. S. Worcester Collection 1975.582

Bourdon was a founder of the Academy, and from 1652–54 he served as painter to the court of Queen Christine of Sweden. Born in the Protestant city of Montpellier, he was apprenticed at an early age to the Parisian painter Josias Barthelémy. The haunting portrait reproduced here is a perfect embodiment of Bourdon's artistic principles. He used the soberest of colors, and few of them. With superb drawing he created a work of restraint, intelligence, and nobility.

25 Meindert Hobbema, *1638–1709* *Dutch*

The Watermill with the Great Red Roof, c. 1670
Oil on canvas. 32 x 43⅛ in (81.3 x 109.6 cm)
Gift of Mr. and Mrs. Frank G. Logan 1894.1031

Hobbema, Ruisdael's finest pupil, is the great Dutch landscapist of the Baroque period, a painter of sensibility who was aware of the effects of natural phenomena on man. His use of color and the quality of his brushwork place him among the great landscape painters of Holland.

[26] Claude Gellée (Le Lorrain), *1600–82 French*

Landscape with Sacrificial Procession, 1673
Oil on canvas. 40 x 50 in (101.7 x 127 cm)
Robert A. Waller Fund 1941.1020

Like his near contemporary, Poussin, Claude spent most of his professional career in Rome and greatly influenced subsequent Roman landscape painters. He found his inspiration in the deserted Roman Forum and the surrounding countryside, on the sites of ancient villas, amidst vast panoramas often stretching to infinity. To some of his admirers, his landscapes seemed like the visual counterpart of the works of the poet Vergil.

Claude Gellée
Study of Trees
White gouache over black chalk on tan paper
The Frances A. Elkins Memorial Fund 1956.1218

[27] Giuseppe Maria Crespi (*called* Lo Spagnolo), *1665–1747 Italian*

The Marriage at Cana, c. 1685
Oil on canvas. 74 x 97¾ in (188 x 248.4 cm)
Wirt D. Walker Fund 1956.129

This early canvas by the great Bolognese painter reflects his absorbed reaction to what he had seen of Ceronese and Tintoretto during his student days in Venice. Crespi gained great fame as a muralist and painter of religious and mythological scenes and was commissioned to do pictures of Prince Eugène of Savoy and the Grand Duke Ferdinand of Tuscany.

27

29

28 Antoine Watteau, *1684–1721* *French*

The Dreamer
Oil on panel. 9⅛ x 6¾ in (23.2 x 17.1 cm)
Mr. and Mrs. L. L. Coburn Fund 1960.305

Watteau represents the early eighteenth-century French paintings that were strongly influenced by the Flemish masters, Rubens in particular. Such paintings appealed enormously to the French collectors of the period. *The Dreamer* is a splendidly moving specimen of the intimate scenes of which Watteau was an accomplished master—these small treasures, perfect in their surfaces and use of colors and forms, evoke a curiously melancholy mood.

29 John Singleton Copley, *1738–1815* *American-British*

Mrs. Daniel Hubbard (Mary Greene), c. 1764
Oil on canvas. 50¼ x 39⅞ in (127.7 x 101.3 cm)
Art Institute Purchase Fund 1947.28

Copley based this portrait of an assured member of the Boston mercantile aristocracy on a mezzotint of an English noblewoman. The sober style he developed during his American years—the work of his later English period is more sophisticated—is remarkably appropriate. His intense observation and his meticulous care in execution enable his portrait of Mrs. Hubbard to triumph over the somewhat inconsistent artificiality of his sources.

Antoine Watteau
The Old Savoyard
Red and black chalk
The Helen Regenstein Collection
1964.73

30

31

30 François Boucher, *1703–70* *French*

Pense-t-il aux Raisins?, 1747
Oil on canvas. 31⅝ x 27 in (80.0 x 68.5 cm)
Purchased from Martha E. Leverone Bequest
1973.304

Boucher, the perfect painter and master of the playful, exhibits both aspects of his formidable talent in this enchanting painting. Boy, girl, and child are elegantly observed and slightly stylized. The landscape is generalized but based on a strict study of nature. It is the animals that are rendered with the greatest realism. The mood the painter evokes is one of pastoral poetry.

31 Jean-Baptiste Oudry, *1686–1755* *French*

Still Life with Monkey, Fruits and Flowers, 1724
Oil on canvas. 56 x 57 in (142.2 x 144.3 cm)
Major Acquisitions Centennial Fund 1977.486

This example of the artist's Rococo style of the 1720s was painted when he was at the peak of his career. It is one of Oudry's most important and most original still lifes. Here he shows not only his usual quality as a sensitive painter of animals, but his mastery of the traditional elements of still life—flowers, fruit, and plate.

François Boucher
Boy with a Carrot
Pastel
The Helen Regenstein Collection 1971.22

[32] Giovanni Battista Tiepolo,
1696–1770 Italian

Rinaldo Enchanted by Armida, c. 1755
Oil on canvas. 73½ x 84½ in (186.9 x 214.6 cm)
Gift of James Deering 1925.700

Tiepolo was the last major old master of Venice and the greatest monumental decorator of his century. In this painting Tiepolo illustrates a scene from Tasso's *Jerusalem Delivered,* a romantic epic dealing with the First Crusade, in which the pagan Armida entices the Christian Rinaldo and holds up the capture of Jerusalem. The landscape is reminiscent of an old-fashioned stage decoration. The methods and outlook are similar to those used by Tiepolo in dealing with sacred themes.

33

33 Francesco Guardi, *1712–93* *Italian*

The Grand Canal, Venice, c. 1745
Oil on canvas. 28¾ x 47 in (75.6 x 119.4 cm)
Wirt D. Walker Fund 1951.21

Guardi excelled at painting theatrical views of Venice. He had an eye for the picturesque that seems to anticipate the later Romantic and Impressionist painters. This brilliant view of Venice on a shimmering day, with the commerce of the city visible, is one of his finest works. The cool coloration is a bit surprising, but on certain days the city does have the very tonalities that the painter has given it.

Francesco Guardi
Capriccio: Gateway near a Landing Bridge
Pen and brown ink with brown wash over pencil
The Helen Regenstein Collection 1969.310

34

34 J.A.D. Ingres, *1780–1867* *French*

Amédée-David, Marquis de Pastoret, 1826
Oil on canvas. 39⅜ x 32¼ in (99.5 x 82.0 cm)
Dorothy Eckhart Williams Bequest, Robert Allerton Purchase Fund,
Bertha E. Brown Fund, Major Acquisitions Fund 1971.452

Ingres was France's most illustrious portrait artist during the first half of the nineteenth century and indeed one of the greatest of all time. Although he seems to adhere strictly to reality, one notes that his painting actually deviates markedly from mere appearances. A careful scrutiny of the painting shows that the marquis has an impossibly long neck and that Ingres has lengthened his rather stubby fingers, presumably for the sake of elegance. Ingres seems to treat his portraits as if they were still lifes.

Jacques-Louis David
Portrait of Jeanbon Saint-André
Pen and ink, brown ink, heightened with white, on ivory paper
The Helen Regenstein Collection
1973.153

35 Jacques-Louis David, *1748–1825* *French*

La Marquise de Pastoret, c. 1791–92
Oil on canvas. 52⅜ x 39⅜ in (133.1 x 100.0 cm)
Clyde M. Carr Fund 1967.228

The moral passion and ethical concepts that dominate many of David's paintings are put aside in this portrait of a noble subject in a moment of serene domesticity. The painting is done in David's usual "soft" or blotchy style, without the seemingly airbrushed finish the artist usually employed. This portrait was found in David's studio at the time of his death and was purchased at that time by the son of the lady pictured.

35

36

37

36 Francisco Goya y Lucientes, *1746–1828 Spanish*

Portrait of General José Manuel Romero, c. 1810
Oil on canvas. 41½ x 34½ in (105.5 x 83.5 cm)
Gift of Charles Deering McCormick 1970.1036

Goya was a supreme portraitist and capable of flattering his sitters. What catches the viewer off-guard, however, is that, deprived of the benefits of modern medicine and dentistry, his subjects often give a grotesque impression. Isolated in mid-life to total deafness, Goya was a complicated and difficult man, but his consummate professionalism is not to be ignored.

37 Jean Honoré Fragonard, *1732–1806 French*

Portrait of a Man as Don Quixote, c. 1769
Oil on canvas. 31¾ x 25½ in (80.7 x 64.8 cm)
Gift of Mary and Leigh Block in honor of John Maxon 1977.123

Fragonard epitomizes the French spirit—its finesse, vivacity, and charming brilliance. Although he worked for a time with Boucher, who aroused in him an interest in decorative painting, he was attracted by the work of Rubens and Rembrandt, and their influences can be seen here. But he has his own characteristic manner—a rapid, impulsive style, with subtle line. In this beautiful portrait (one of a series), Fragonard might have been thinking of Cervantes himself—it is known that he was acquainted with his novel and planned to illustrate it one day.

Jean Honoré Fragonard
The Letter (or *The Spanish Conversation*), brown wash over pencil
The Margaret Day Blake Collection
1945.32

38 Eugène Delacroix, *1798–1863* *French*

Combat between the Giaour and the Pasha
Oil on canvas.
22½ x 28 in (57.2 x 71.1 cm)
Gift of Mrs. Bertha Palmer Thorne,
Mrs. Rose Movius Palmer,
Mr. and Mrs. Arthur M. Wood,
Mr. and Mrs. Gordon Palmer 1962.966

This famous picture was inspired by a poem of Byron's. It is a prototype of a French Romantic painting and is the artist's finest early canvas. Reacting to the cool classicism of David and Ingres, Delacroix turned to Romantic themes, elaborately conceived and rich in action, and based on historical or literary subjects. The superbly drawn *Combat between the Giaour and the Pasha* expresses both vitality and color.

Eugène Delacroix
Sheet of Animal Studies and sketches for "Cromwell in Windsor Castle," pencil, pen and ink, watercolor
David Adler Fund 1971.309

39 J. M. W. Turner, *1775–1851* *English*

Valley of Aosta—Snowstorm, Avalanche, and Thunderstorm, 1836–37
Oil on canvas. 36¼ x 48 in (92.1 x 122.0 cm)
Frederick T. Haskell Collection Fund 1947.513

Though Turner looked back to Claude and Wilson, he became the foremost example of English Romantic art and one of the formative influences on painters after him. From the 1830s on he was primarily concerned with the painting of light—the ostensible subject matter took only second place. While this painting was executed from sketches and watercolors made in the Italian Alps, it has the intensity and impact of an immediate experience.

40 Gustave Courbet, *1819–77* *French*

Mère Grégoire, 1855
Oil on canvas. 50¾ x 38¼ in (128.9 x 97.2 cm)
Wilson L. Mead Fund 1930.78

In this work of Courbet's early maturity, he has painted a straightforward and uncompromising portrait of the Swiss *patronne* of the Brasserie Andler as she sits making change and offering a flower to a favorite customer. He exhibits a technical finesse which, for all his characteristic rebelliousness, derives from earlier masters. Nor does he escape the humanistic passion of the Romantics, despite his professed antipathy toward the essential elements in their view.

41 Jean François Millet, *1814–75* *French*

Horse, c. 1841
Oil on canvas. 65½ x 77½ in (166.4 x 196.8 cm)
Charles H. and Mary F. S. Worcester Collection 1976.30

This large and impressive picture was said to have been commissioned as an ensign for a veterinary. The image of the animal is so heroic and monumental that at first sight the viewer fails to notice the finesse with which the landscape is painted and the delicate touches in the human figure. Millet belongs to the mainstream of the French tradition. His technique derives from Fragonard and beyond him to Salvator Rosa and the painters of seventeenth-century Italy.

40

41

42

42 Gustave Courbet, *1819–77* *French*

The Rock at Hautpierre, c. 1869
Oil on canvas. 31½ x 39½ in (80.2 x 100.3 cm)
Emily Crane Chadbourne Fund 1967.140

Courbet returned often to Ornans, his birthplace near the Swiss border, to paint the scenery. For a time he copied the work of the Spanish and Dutch painters, especially Rembrandt. Yet he struggled hard to express his concepts of reality in his own way. This superb landscape shows the classic structural quality that was admired so much by Cézanne.

43 Edouard Manet, *1832–83* *French*

Still Life with Carp, 1864
Oil on canvas. 28⅞ x 36¼ in (73.4 x 92.1 cm)
Mr. and Mrs. L. L. Coburn Memorial Collection 1942.311

Though this painting clearly derives from Chardin, Manet has in no way merely emulated his style. The technique and color are clearly his own. His drawing technique may occasionally be tentative, but he is always successful in communicating a sense of formal structure. In this early work there are intimations of Monet's later manner: he lightened his palette and pushed his own innovations forward; yet he remained solidly grounded in traditionalism.

43

44

45

44 Edouard Manet, *1832–83* *French*

Christ Mocked, 1865
Oil on canvas. 75⅛ x 58⅜ in (190.8 x 148.3 cm)
Gift of James Deering 1925.703

Manet, who shocked his contemporaries as a radical painter, was, in fact, a most conservative artist, full of knowledge of the past and dependent upon the classic tradition. This canvas evokes the early Velasquez—it is a mid-nineteenth-century restatement of a Spanish Baroque religious piece. Manet seems to be remembering his own fate in Christ's. The man in the yellow turban bears a remarkable resemblance to Clemenceau whose portrait Manet painted twice that year.

45 Frédéric Bazille, *1841–70* *French*

Self Portrait, 1865
Oil on canvas. 42¾ x 28⅜ in (108.6 x 72.0 cm)
Frank H. and Louise B. Woods Purchase Fund
1962.336

Bazille's death in the Franco-Prussian War cut short the career of one of the most competent Impressionists. His talent was prodigious, and his capacities for precise observation were formidable. In this painting, he suggests the skin tone beneath the sleeve with fantastic technical mastery, through direct paint. It is hard to categorize his work—it bears a resemblance to Monet, or the young Pissarro, and yet Bazille has a straightforward sobriety which makes him refreshingly individual.

Edouard Manet
Portrait of Berthe Morisot
Watercolor
The Helen Regenstein Collection
1963.812

46 Winslow Homer, *1836–1910* *American*

Croquet Scene, 1866
Oil on canvas. 15⅞ x 26¹⁄₁₆ in (40.3 x 66.2 cm)
Friends of American Art Collection 1942.35

The strong narrative quality of Homer's painting could well be attributed to his early years as a journalist. Though he began his career as a lithographer and magazine illustrator, he made his reputation during the Civil War as an artist-reporter for *Harper's Weekly.* His work remained largely free of European influences, despite visits to France and England. In *Croquet Scene* we see the simplicity of composition and relationships of isolated shapes that are characteristic of Homer's mature style.

47 James Abbott McNeill Whistler, *1834–1903* *American*

The Artist in His Studio, c. 1867–68
Oil on wood. 24¾ x 18¾ in (63.0 x 47.7 cm)
Friends of American Art Collection 1912.141

In 1867–68, Whistler considered painting a large studio picture portraying himself, his models, and his friends Fantin-Latour and Albert Moore—a theme no doubt inspired by similar works done by Fantin and Courbet. The final picture was never executed, but the artist did make two oil studies, one belonging to the Art Institute, the other to the City of Dublin Art Gallery. Whistler's aesthetic credo may be considered a creative act in itself. "Art should be independent of all claptrap," he wrote, "[it] should stand alone, and appeal to the artistic sense of eye or ear, without confounding this with emotions entirely foreign to it."

46

47

48 Claude Monet, *1840–1926* *French*

The Beach at Sainte Adresse, 1867
Oil on canvas. 29½ x 39¾ in (75.0 x 101.0 cm)
Mr. and Mrs. L. L. Coburn Memorial Collection 1933.439

Cézanne is said to have remarked of Monet, "Only an eye, but my God, what an eye!" Here one sees the direct and simple way in which the young artist records a natural scene. The drawing is clear, and color and light are rendered in simple and directly painted patches of pure color. He strives (as he himself puts it) to represent "that which lies between the object and the artist . . . the beauty of the atmosphere—the impossible."

49 Claude Monet, *1840–1926* *French*

The River, 1868
Oil on canvas. 31⅞ x 39½ in (81.0 x 100.3 cm)
Potter Palmer Collection 1922.427

This early Monet shows the artist's mistress, Camille, sitting placidly on the banks of the Seine. It is difficult to see how this radiant and serene scene could ever have been considered revolutionary—it was Monet's concern with conveying an atmosphere and evoking a mood, of course, that amounted to a startling departure from artistic tradition. His aim was not to depict detail but to paint subjectively what he saw.

48

49

50

50 Claude Monet, *1840–1926* *French*

Old St. Lazare Station, Paris, 1877
Oil on canvas. 23½ x 31½ in (59.6 x 80.2 cm)
Mr. and Mrs. Martin A. Ryerson Collection
1933.1158

Even the interior of a train shed, Monet thought, could be a suitable subject for a painting. Here the artist is able to convey a real sense of the station and the open space beyond, not just through the actual perspective drawing but especially through his rendering of the steam from the locomotives as it obscures the view of the world beyond. The human beings are merely dabs of paint, yet each stroke in the painting serves to convey a tacitly understood set of forms.

[51] Claude Monet, *1840–1926* *French*

Iris by the Pond, 1919–25
Oil on canvas. 79 x 79½ in (200.7 x 201.9 cm)
Art Institute Purchase Fund 1956.1202

Monet's famous water-lily pictures engaged him for nearly a quarter of a century. In most of his late work he explored the fusion of real and reflected light on the surface of his little water-lily pond. This painting is almost a hallucination of light and color on water, flowers, and foliage. There is an explosion of impressions that reaches forward into Expressionism.

51

52

52 Jean-Baptiste Camille Corot, *1796–1875* *French*

Interrupted Reading, c. 1865 or 1870
Oil on canvas. 36½ x 25¾ in (92.8 x 65.5 cm)
Potter Palmer Collection 1922.410

Corot's figure paintings rank among his most impressive achievements, and canvases such as this were done for his own pleasure as a painter. They demonstrate the problem that so completely absorbs the traditional artist: how to organize forms in space in terms of color and pattern to preserve the illusion of air, space, and solid forms and—paradoxically—the sense of the flatness of the surface upon which the painting is executed.

53 Gustave Caillebotte, *1848–94* *French*

Paris, a Rainy Day, 1877
Oil on canvas. 83½ x 108¾ in (212.2 x 276.2 cm)
Charles H. and Mary F. S. Worcester Collection
1964.336

Caillebotte was a friend and patron of the Impressionists and indeed one of the first to buy their works. This canvas, which interestingly enough predated the *Grand Jatte* by a few years, is his masterpiece, and the brilliance with which he constructed his design reflects the discipline he acquired as an engineer. The observation is subtle. Only with careful examination is it clear how carefully and almost rigidly the painting is composed.

53

54

54 Camille Pissarro, *1830/1–1903* *French*

The Crystal Palace, 1871
Oil on canvas. 18½ x 28$\frac{3}{16}$ in (47 x 73.2 cm)
Gift of Mr. and Mrs. B. E. Bensinger 1972.1164

Impressed by Manet and his circle, Pissarro joined them and exhibited with them from 1874 to 1886. For a brief period shortly after 1885, he worked with the pointillist methods of Seurat, but only with limited success. His work is perhaps closest to that of Monet, but his forms are muted and more diffuse, and he paints in heavier textures with a more caressing brushstroke.

55 Pierre Auguste Renoir, *1841–1919* *French*

Lady at the Piano, c. 1875
Oil on canvas. 36¾ x 29¼ in (93.4 x 74.3 cm)
Mr. and Mrs. Martin A. Ryerson Collection 1937.1025

In the first phase of Renoir's mature style he painted familiar scenes from everyday life—pretty women and children of the rich bourgeoisie. This painting was shown in the second Impressionist exhibition of 1875. Renoir's loose but careful brushwork is applied to conventional techniques of academic drawing. The way in which the white background always shows through the paint is, however, a triumph of Renoir's individual method.

55

56 Pierre Auguste Renoir,
1841–1919 French

The Rowers' Lunch, c. 1879 or 1880
Oil on canvas. 21½ x 25¾ in (54.7 x 65.5 cm)
Potter Palmer Collection 1922.437

A large version of this picture is in the Phillips Collection in Washington. By the time this painting was done Renoir had become a consummate master of scale. Though the reproduction suggests a much larger picture, almost life-sized, the painting is in fact just over two feet wide. The picture was a special favorite of Mrs. Palmer's and was acquired after her friendship with Mary Cassatt brought the works of the Impressionists to her attention.

Auguste Renoir
Study for "The Bathers," pencil and colored chalks touched with brush
Bequest of Kate L. Brewster 1949.514

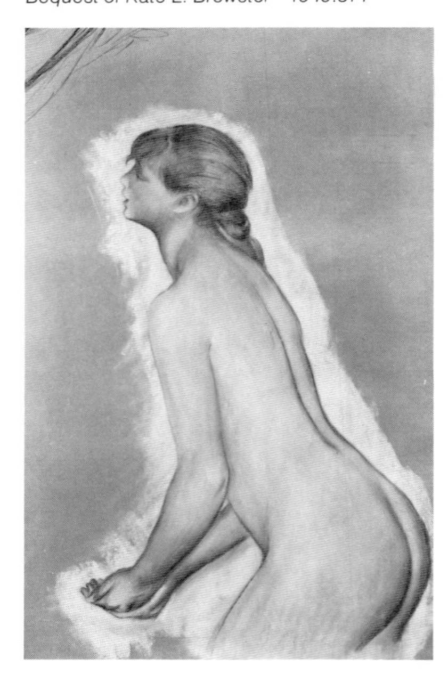

56

57

57 Pierre Auguste Renoir, *1841–1919* *French*

Two Little Circus Girls, 1879
Oil on canvas. 51½ x 38¾ in (130.9 x 98.5 cm)
Potter Palmer Collection 1922.440

In its simplicity and genuine charm, this painting must rank as one of Renoir's masterpieces. It was, incidentally, Mrs. Palmer's favorite picture, and she kept it with her always. The Wartenburg sisters are shown here at the beginning of their careers as circus jugglers. Here we see Renoir at his very best—making use of his chinaware painter's technique, but not yet influenced by his desire to emulate old masters.

58 Pierre Auguste Renoir, *1841–1919* *French*

On the Terrace, 1881
Oil on canvas. 39½ x 31⅞ in (100.3 x 81 cm)
Mr. and Mrs. L. L. Coburn Memorial Collection 1933.455

This picture is probably the most popular of the Art Institute's Impressionist paintings. It is a straightforward and winning likeness of a pretty woman and her pretty daughter. The artist has magnificently conveyed the radiance and glow of a warm and beautiful day in France. Somber subjects did not find their way into Renoir's repertoire.

60

59 John Singer Sargent,
1856–1925 American

Mrs. Charles Gifford Dyer (May Anthony), 1880
Oil on canvas. 24⅝ x 17¼ in (62.7 x 43.9 cm)
Friends of American Art Collection 1915.592

Mrs. Dyer, the subject of this painting, was the wife of the American artist and lived the greater part of her life abroad. She and her husband were close friends of Sargent and spent a good deal of time with him when they were in Venice. One senses Sargent's close relationship with the sitter. Here his incredibly facile technique is enhanced by an arresting style and depth of psychological penetration that are absent from some of his later portraits.

60 William M. Harnett,
1848–92 American

For Sunday's Dinner (Still Life), 1888
Oil on canvas. 37⅛ x 21⅛ in (94.3 x 53.8 cm)
Wilson L. Mead Fund 1958.296

Harnett never achieved a better still life. The simple subject masks the complex composition of verticals, horizontals, and diagonals, the dramatic interplay of textures, and the subtle use of color. His use of light and shadow places an emphasis upon the worn hinges and lock of the old cupboard, endowing the scene with a sense of heightened reality and personal history.

61

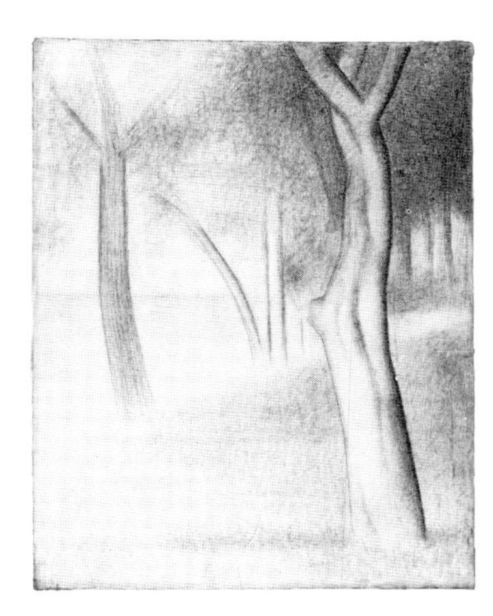

Georges Seurat
Landscape with Trees, conté crayon
The Helen Regenstein Collection
1966.184

61 Georges Seurat, *1859–91* *French*

Sunday Afternoon on the Island of La Grande Jatte, 1884–86
Oil on canvas. 81 x 120⅜ in (205.7 x 305.8 cm)
Helen Birch Bartlett Memorial Collection
1926.224

Seurat's pointillism was based on his studies of optical theory. He tried here to convey the flickering light of a summer Sunday by dots of color which, when seen from a distance, could be reconstructed by the eye into shapes and forms. The design is arbitrary and rendered as an enigmatically austere tableau, motionless yet paradoxically filled with life. Felix Fénéon described the painting in *La Vogue:* "Seurat has treated his forty or so figures in summary and hieratic style, setting them up frontally or with their backs to us or in profile, seated at right-angles, stretched out horizontally, or bolt upright: like a Puvis de Chavannes gone modern."

62

63

62 Edgar Degas, *1834–1917 French*

Woman in a Rose Hat, 1879
Pastel, tempera, and oil on canvas. 33¾ x 29⅝ in (85.8 x 75.3 cm)
Joseph Winterbotham Collection 1954.325

The portrait for which this sketch was made was presumably destroyed. When Mme Dietz-Monin, who had grown impatient with sitting, offered to send Degas her hat and boa instead, he replied, "Let us leave the portrait alone, I beg of you. I was so surprised by your letter suggesting that I reduce it to a boa and hat that I shall not answer you.... Must I tell you that I regret having started something in my own manner only to find myself transforming it completely into yours."

63 Edgar Degas, *1834–1917 French*

The Millinery Shop, c. 1882
Oil on canvas. 39⅛ x 43⅜ in (99.5 x 110.3 cm)
Mr. and Mrs. L. L. Coburn Memorial Collection 1933.428

This is one of the painter's finest works, in which his sense of design, form, and color, as well as his familiarity with Japanese prints and with the art of the past, combine to make a haunting image in time and space. The seemingly casual design is brilliantly constructed. More than a casual and trivial domestic scene, this painting established Degas as the last great master of the old tradition.

64

[64] Edgar Degas, *1834–1917* *French*

Dancers in the Wings, c. 1890
Pastel on board. 25½ x 19½ in (64.8 x 49.5 cm)
Mr. and Mrs. Martin A. Ryerson Collection 1937.1032

Unlike the Impressionist painters who dissolved all forms in light and atmosphere, Degas was primarily concerned with line and motion. The ballet, of course, was one of his favorite subjects, and he recorded his impressions of dancers both on and off the stage. *Dancers in the Wings* is typical of his behind-the-scenes works. The informal pose, the adjusting of a costume reflect the mundane reality behind the beautiful illusion about to be presented on stage.

[65] Paul Cézanne, *1839–1906* *French*

Mme Cézanne in Yellow Chair, 1893–95
Oil on canvas. 31⅞ x 25½ in (81.0 x 64.8 cm)
Wilson L. Mead Fund 1948.54

Cézanne's long-suffering wife was his favorite model, since she alone was willing to submit to the hours of motionlessness he required of his subjects. In the process of fixing his gaze on her, he had managed to transfer his intensity so that she *seems* totally absorbed. His method here is slow and laborious—he adjusts his paint strokes to describe the effects of light and to relate them to an over-all pictorial structure.

65

Edgar Degas
Four Studies of a Jockey, essence and gouache
Mr. and Mrs. Lewis L. Coburn Collection 1933.469

66

66 Paul Cézanne, *1839–1906 French*

The Basket of Apples, c. 1895
Oil on canvas. 25¾ x 32 in (65.4 x 81.3 cm)
Helen Birch Bartlett Memorial Collection
1926.252

In this painting, the viewer can see the fullest manifestation of Cézanne's method—each brushstroke is executed with complete regard for its impact. The still life was a genre that permitted the artist's utter concentration. There is a sense of timeless solidity which bursts forth in glowing color. His method of drawing and departure from the appearance of reality give the viewer a sense of monumental scale that is related to his achievement in landscape.

Paul Cézanne
Pistachio Tree at the Château Noir, watercolor
Mr. and Mrs. Martin A. Ryerson Collection
1937.1030

67 Paul Cézanne, *1839–1906* *French*

Vase of Tulips, 1890–92
Oil on canvas. 23½ x 16⅝ in (59.6 x 42.3 cm)
Mr. and Mrs. L. L. Coburn Memorial Collection 1933.423

In this painting Cézanne makes fragile garden flowers seem both delicate and eternally solid. He always enjoyed doing still lifes, for they permitted him to make the most minute observations and adjustments in his work. Here his method of drawing and composition achieves the soberest and grandest of results. The motionlessness of the subject does not prevent Cézanne from achieving a liveliness of touch and reality that is an intense evocation of nature.

68 Mary Cassatt, *1844–1926* *American*

The Bath, c. 1891–92
Oil on canvas. 39½ x 26 in (100.3 x 66.1 cm)
Robert A. Waller Fund 1910.2

Cassatt was one of those unusual people who continued to learn—though fragile health limited her after the early 1890s. Here she commands all she has gained from Degas and the Japanese printmakers. The result is an extraordinary quality of line, decoratively and functionally used. An intimate moment of existence is presented with coolness and taste.

Mary Cassatt
Corner of the Sofa, pencil
The Margaret Day Blake Collection
1967.145

67

68

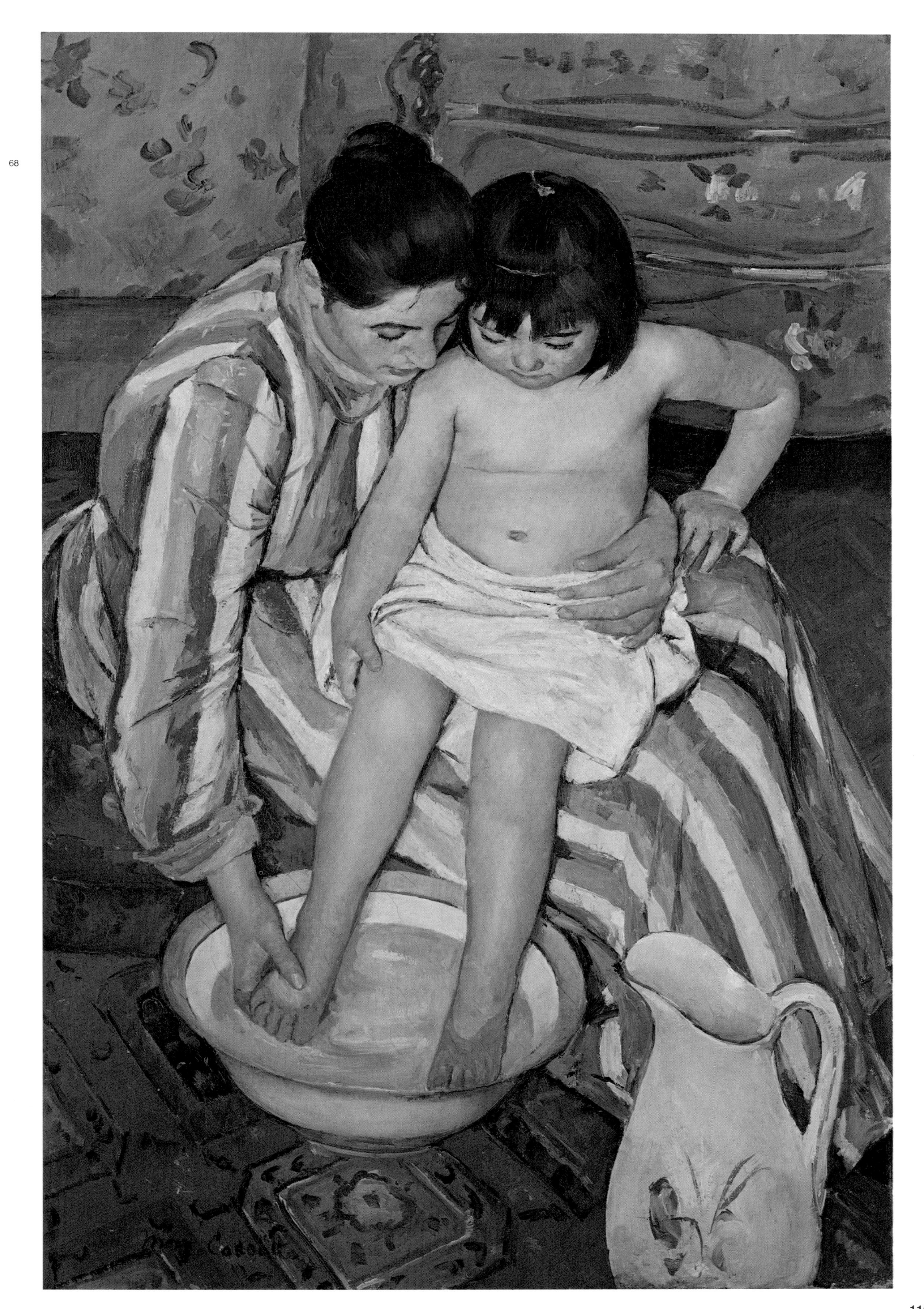

69 Vincent van Gogh, *1853–90* *Dutch*

Bedroom at Arles, 1888
Oil on canvas. 28¾ x 36 in (73.0 x 91.5 cm)
Helen Birch Bartlett Memorial Collection
1926.417

Van Gogh said of this picture that it showed solidity, coziness, and quiet. He said he wanted it as "simple as Seurat . . . with heavy thick paint." It is a memorable image, and its extended perspective makes it a haunting and haunted painting. A plain ordinary interior of scrubbed, respectable poverty is captivatingly endowed with freshness. Van Gogh turns the tricks of perspective to serve his own use and convey a rich intensity of meaning.

70 Vincent van Gogh, *1853–90* *Dutch*

Self Portrait, 1886–88
Oil on cardboard. 16½ x 13¼ in (42.0 x 33.7 cm)
Joseph Winterbotham Collection 1954.326

This is one of the twenty-four self portraits painted during Van Gogh's stay with his brother in Paris, 1886–88. It reflects his fascination with the pointillist theories of Pissarro and Seurat, whose work he greatly admired. He has broken out of the cool and objective style of the pointillists, however, loosening and lengthening his strokes and thus producing a more expressive and emotional effect. Van Gogh's superlative color and mastery of drawing are much in evidence here.

70

71 Henri de Toulouse-Lautrec,
1854–1901 French

At the Moulin Rouge, 1892
Oil on canvas. 48⅜ x 55¼ in (122.9 x 140.4 cm)
Helen Birch Bartlett Memorial Collection
1928.610

In this painting of the most popular Parisian dance hall of the 1890s, Toulouse-Lautrec shifts his attention from the dance floor to the spectators. This is not only one of Toulouse's most famous works but very possibly his best. The care, daring, and brilliance of his perceptions are expressed here with unquestioned technical supremacy.

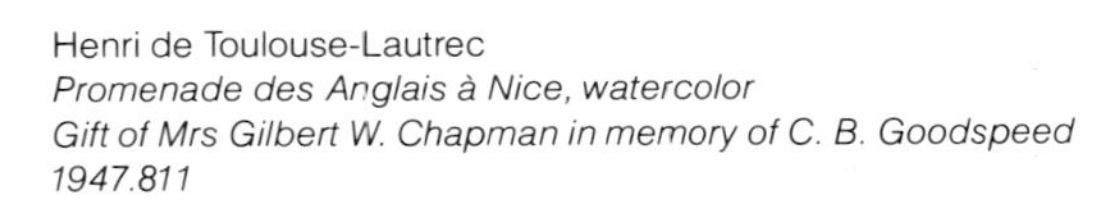

Henri de Toulouse-Lautrec
Promenade des Anglais à Nice, watercolor
Gift of Mrs Gilbert W. Chapman in memory of C. B. Goodspeed
1947.811

71

72

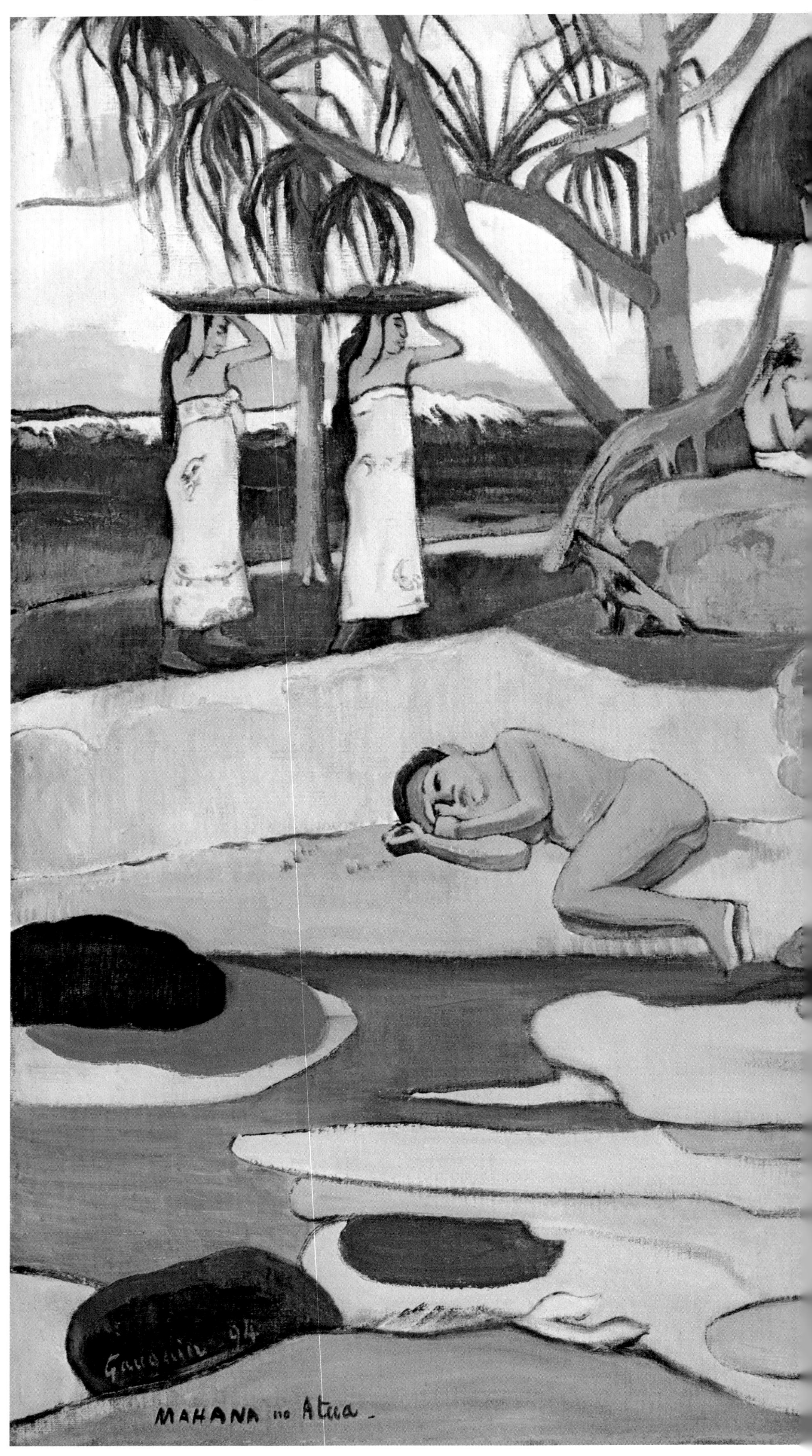

72 Paul Gauguin, *1848–1903* *French*

The Day of the God, 1894
Oil on canvas. 27⅜ x 35⅝ in (69.6 x 90.5 cm)
Helen Birch Bartlett Memorial Collection
1926.198

Although this painting was in fact executed in Paris, it epitomizes Gauguin's fascination with the South Seas. His highly decorative manner of painting is a unique adaptation to his Impressionist origins and his own feelings and interests. Let no one dismiss him as a primitive, however. He is always the complete professional, ever in command and supported by consummate technical skill.

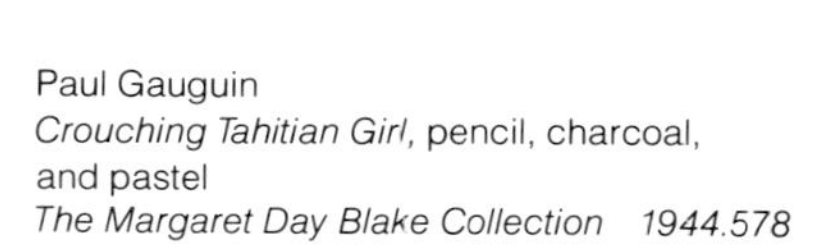
Paul Gauguin
Crouching Tahitian Girl, pencil, charcoal, and pastel
The Margaret Day Blake Collection 1944.578

73 Thomas Eakins, *1844–1916* *American*

Addie, Woman in Black, 1899
Oil on canvas. 24 x 20 in (61.0 x 50.9 cm)
Friends of American Art Collection 1939.548

Mary Adeline Williams was an intimate friend of the Eakins family and subsequently a member of the household. She was a patient subject for Eakins in his later years. In this painting, technique is obviously subordinate to the faithful portrayal of the subject. Honesty, sobriety, and seriousness are more important here than any effort to convey prettiness or charm. It is evident that Eakins's exposure to the Spanish Baroque masters had a lasting influence on him.

74 Maurice de Vlaminck, *1876–1958* *French*

Houses at Chatou, 1905–6
Oil on canvas. 32 x 39⅞ in (81.3 x 101.3 cm)
Gift of Maurice E. Culberg 1951.19

In 1905, the paintings of Matisse, Derain, Vlaminck, and their friends were considered shocking to conservative museum-goers, and the term *les fauves,* or "wild beasts," seemed like an apt description. The starting point of fauvism, Matisse later said, was "the courage to return to the purity of means." Vlaminck painted a number of canvases of remarkable compositional sophistication around Chatou, and this is one of his best. The mosaic form suggests the method of Van Gogh, with whom he worked closely from the autumn of 1905.

74

75 Georges Braque, *1882–1963 French*

Harbor in Normandy, 1909
Oil on canvas. 31⅞ x 31⅞ in (81 x 81 cm)
Samuel A. Marx Purchase Fund 1970.98

In this superb example of Braque's Cubist technique, the painter's task is arduous: to dissect a remembered visual impression and reconstruct a pictorial equivalent. Cézanne's influence is apparent in the layering of myriad passages of color to reflect light and depth and yet emphasize the flatness of the surface. Braque wrote of this painting, "What especially attracted me—and what was the main preoccupation of Cubism—was the materialization of that new space which I sensed."

76 Robert Delaunay, *1882–1941 French*

Champ de Mars, the Red Tower, 1911
Oil on canvas. 64 x 51½ in (162.6 x 130.9 cm)
Joseph Winterbotham Collection 1959.1

On the back of this picture Delaunay inscribed a telling phrase—*époque destructive*—a clue to his conception of the Cubist idiom. He is attempting the destruction of form as it is normally experienced and understood. The fragmenting of the shapes of the building gives the painting a sense of dynamism and modernity. Delaunay is interested in testing the effects of color and motion, yet he paints in a tasteful, elegant way that produces a highly decorative canvas.

75

76

77

[77] Wassily Kandinsky, *1866–1944* *Russian*

Improvisation with Green Center, No. 176, *c.* 1913
Oil on canvas. 43¼ x 47½ in (109.9 x 120.6 cm)
Arthur Jerome Eddy Memoral Collection 1931.510

Kandinsky is generally thought of as the founder of non-representational art. His first abstract work, a watercolor, was painted in 1911. Originally an economist, he was briefly influenced by the Impressionists and the Fauves, but shortly turned to free play with colors and two-dimensional forms. By displaying painted areas in relation to one another, he gives the spectator an impression of light, movement, and color.

[78] Francis Picabia, *1879–1953* *Spanish*

Edtaonisl, 1913
Oil on canvas. 118¼ x 118⅜ in (300.4 x 301.1 cm)
Gift of Mr. and Mrs. Armand Phillip Bartos
1953.622

Edtaonisl is the second of a group of three canvases painted by Picabia in 1913 and inspired by his impressions on his first trip to America, where he participated in the Armory Show. The title is made up of several words referring to the painter's adventures on the trip. In this painting Picabia tries to re-create the reactions of a Dominican monk as he watches a dance performance on board ship.

79

79 Juan Gris (José Vittorio Gonzales), *1887–1927* *Spanish*

Portrait of Picasso, 1912
Oil on canvas. 29¼ x 36⅞ in (74.3 x 93.7 cm)
Gift of Leigh B. Block 1958.525

It is not difficult to see Juan Gris as an ancestor of modern poster-making and illustration. Born and raised in Madrid, he moved to Paris in 1906, where he joined Picasso and other painters of the avant-garde. His own style of Cubism, however, was more severe and more lucid than the Analytic Cubist painting of Braque and Picasso. Color is virtually abandoned, and the palette is restricted to the extremes of blacks and whites. Here we see the typical Cubist disjunction of planes, yet the vivid definition of edges gives the form solidarity and precision.

80 Giorgio de Chirico, *1888–1934* *Italian*

The Philosopher's Conquest, 1914
Oil on canvas. 49½ x 39¼ in (125.8 x 100.3 cm)
Joseph Winterbotham Collection 1939.405

The boat, factory chimney, train, round tower, clock, and other iconographical images in this painting are common ones in Chirico's works. Images of food, as seen in the foreground, are typical of his still lifes, though the cannon and cannon balls are unique to this painting. The incongruous details he brings together may have no place in the logical world of reality but they stimulate the imagination and the subconscious, where consistency and logic have no place. De Chirico was a pioneer of subconscious expression and a great influence on later surrealism.

G. de Chirico

81

81 Marc Chagall, *1887—* *French*

The Praying Jew
(The Rabbi of Vitebsk), 1914
Oil on canvas. 46 x 35 in (116.9 x 88.9 cm)
Joseph Winterbotham Collection 1937.188

In his earlier work Chagall enjoyed evoking the village life of his childhood and youth. Here the artist makes one of his occasional ventures into realism charged with high flights of imagination. The painting (a second version of which is in the Venetian Museum of Modern Art) is not only one of his most famous works but one of his very finest—a heroic and touching image.

82 Pablo Picasso, *1881–1973* *Spanish*

The Old Guitarist, 1903
Oil on panel, 48⅛ x 32⁷⁄₁₆ in (122.3 x 82.4 cm)
Helen Birch Bartlett Memorial Collection
1926.253

The Old Guitarist is representative of the pictures of Picasso's "blue period," between 1901 and 1904, when he tended to paint downtrodden, pathetic characters who reflected a kind of *fin-de-siècle* despair and isolation. Here the use of blue accentuates the coldness and hunger of the subject. Only the guitar brings some relief to the monochrome and adds warmth and life to the painter's icy palette.

82

Pablo Picasso
Peasant Woman with a Shawl, charcoal on white paper
On extended loan by heirs of Pauline Kohlstaat Palmer
176.57

84

83 Pablo Picasso, *1881–1973* *Spanish*

Daniel-Henry Kahnweiler, 1910
Oil on canvas. 39⅝ x 28⅝ in (100.6 x 72.8 cm)
Gift of Mrs. Gilbert W. Chapman 1948.561

This painting is a major example of Picasso's Analytic Cubist phase in which nature is broken into planes, voids, and solids, with differing aspects shown simultaneously and examined from several points of view, all at once. Though Cézanne was the obvious source for this style, Picasso abandoned the lovely glowing colors of the master and essentially confined himself to raw umber, black, white, and small touches of color.

84 Pablo Picasso, *1881–1973* *Spanish*

Man with a Pipe, 1915
Oil on canvas. 51¼ x 35¼ in (130.3 x 89.5 cm)
Gift of Mrs. Leigh B. Block in memory of Albert D. Lasker 1952.1116

Picasso's experiments with collage are exemplified in this picture, in which pieces of wood, wire, paper, and string are distorted by the artist into a flat composition. The austerity of feeling evoked in Picasso's earlier works in Analytic Cubism is abandoned in this second Cubist phase—often called "Synthetic Cubism"—in which his forms are synthesized and reduced to basic elements and shapes, all in terms of soft, but ravishing color.

[85] Pablo Picasso, *1881–1973* *Spanish*

Mother and Child, 1921
Oil on canvas. 56½ x 64 in (143.5 x 162.6 cm)
Ada Turnbull Hertle Fund,
Mary and Leigh Block Charitable Fund, Inc.,
Mr. and Mrs. Edwin E. Hokin,
Maymar Corporation, Mr. and Mrs. Chauncey McCormick, Mrs. Maurice L. Rothschild
1954.270

A monument of Picasso's own brand of neoclassicism. Taking a stale and shopworn pictorial idiom, Picasso creates a new style by simple pictorial means—earth-colored, broadly brushed drawing. One sees reminiscences of Etruscan mirrors, Greek ceramics, and Hellenistic sculpture. The painting originally included a bearded father to the viewer's left. Picasso eventually cut the figure out in order to allow for intense concentration on mother and child, and later presented the fragment to the Art Institute.

Pablo Picasso
Study for Chicago Civic Center Monument #4, pencil
Gift of the Artist 1968.1054

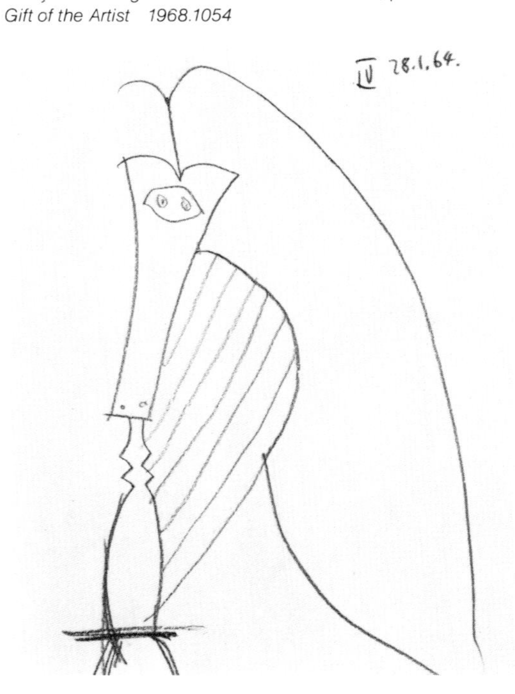

85

86 Henri Matisse, *1869–1954* *French*

Bathers by a River, 1916–17
Oil on canvas. 103 x 154 in (261.6 x 386.1 cm)
Charles H. and Mary F. S. Worcester Collection
1953.158

A heroic, monumental masterpiece by the artist who ranks among the greatest painters of this century. In this canvas Matisse has simplified and altered his forms so that they almost function as symbolic ideograms. Throughout his long career, Matisse summed up and continuously restated the very substance of painting—the re-creation of form and space in terms of colors, values, and lines on a flat suffáce.

Henri Matisse
Self Portrait, lithograph
Gift of Mrs. Homer Hargrave 1964.3

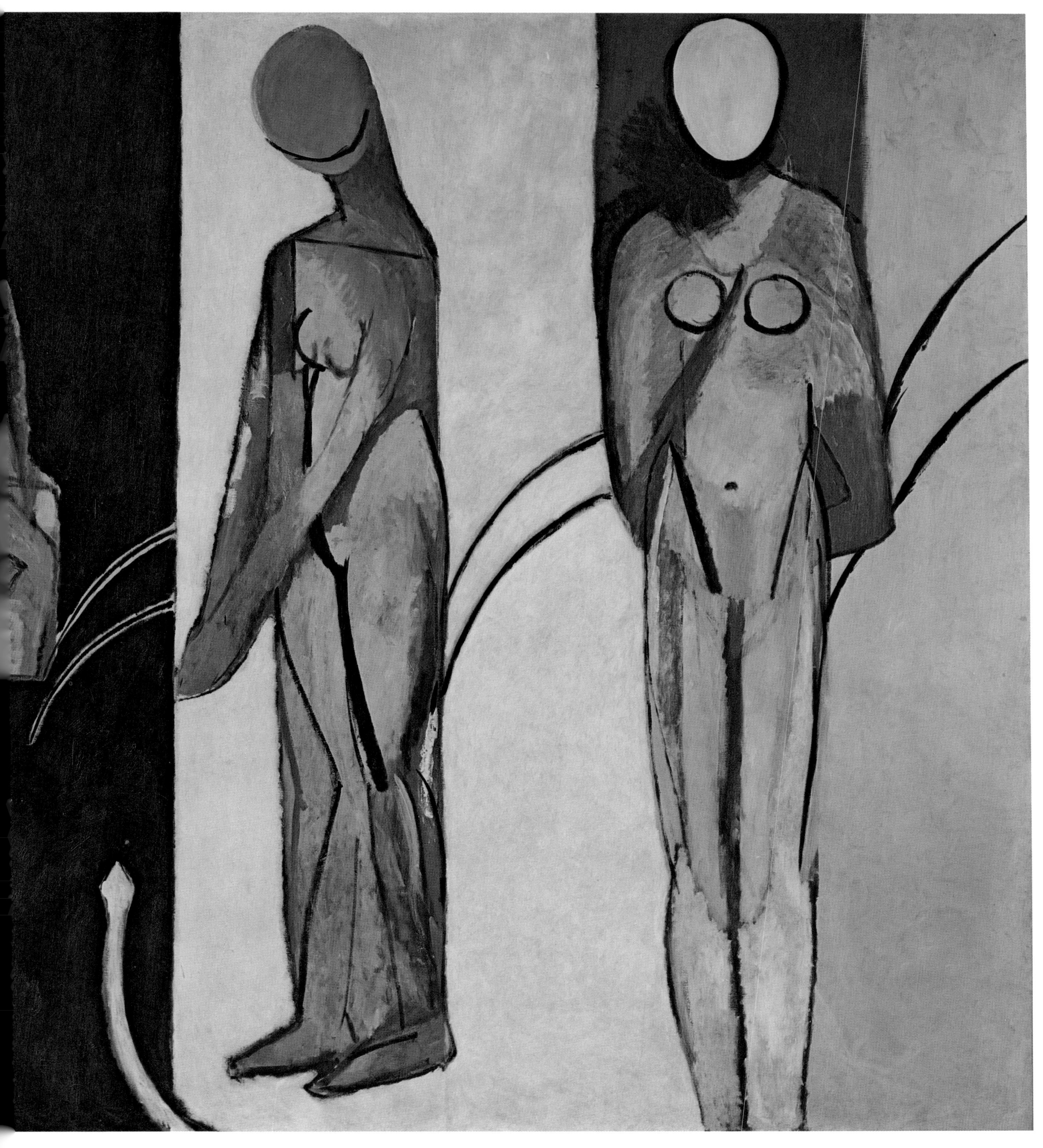

87

88

[87] Henri Matisse, *1869–1954* *French*

Apples, 1916
Oil on canvas. 46 x 35 in (116.9 x 88.9 cm)
Gift of Mrs. Wolfgang Schoenborn and Samuel A. Marx 1948.563

Matisse was the most important painter of the Fauves, to whom color was the most vital element in art. This still life is one of his most monumental, simple, and subtle works. It was painted during a period of his life when he was creating a series of austere masterpieces and making few concessions to prettiness, yet the net result is one of joyous richness. Here the fruit is seen as a generalized symbol rather than as a concrete group of objects in a specific time and place.

[88] Joán Miró, *1893—* *Spanish*

Portrait of a Woman (Juanita Obrador), 1918
Oil on canvas. 27½ x 24½ in (69.5 x 62.0 cm)
Joseph Winterbotham Collection 1957.78

Miró's early training in Barcelona was completely conventional until he met the painter and art dealer Refel Josep Dalman, who introduced him to the work of Picasso and Juan Gris. Their influence can be seen in this portrait. The colors are intense, the patterns bold. The roughly hewn features of the face give it an expression of resignation to some deep, enduring torment.

Henri Matisse
Head of a Girl with Braids, ink and brush
Anonymous gift 1945.194

89 Piet Mondrian, *1872–1944* *Dutch*

Diagonal Composition, 1921
Oil on canvas. $23\frac{5}{8}$ x $23\frac{5}{8}$ in (60.1 x 60.1 cm)
Gift of Edgar Kaufmann, Jr. 1957.307

Mondrian, the outstanding master of nonobjective art in the twentieth century, began his career in Holland as an old-fashioned painter of scenery. In 1910 he went to Paris, where he came into contact with Cubism. Though he first turned to naturalistic subjects, his style developed consistently in the direction of completely abstract expression, in which he achieved the most perfect geometric balances in color, form and line. From 1940 until his death he lived in New York.

90 Georgia O'Keeffe, *1887—* *American*

Black Cross, New Mexico, 1929
Oil on canvas. 39 x $30\frac{1}{16}$ in (99.2 x 76.3 cm)
Art Institute Purchase Fund 1943.95

O'Keeffe studied briefly at the Art Institute. As a young painter she exhibited at "291," the Stieglitz Gallery in New York, and became part of the group that formed there. Later she and Stieglitz were married. Her work has consistently revealed a strength of color and form, and an interest in themes drawn from nature and from the landscape around her home in Abiquiu, near Taos, New Mexico. She seems to reflect the American penchant for iconic, realistic images and formal simplicity.

89

91

91 Grant Wood, *1892–1942* *American*

American Gothic, 1930
Oil on beaverboard. 29⅞ x 24⅞ in (76.0 x 63.3 cm)
Friends of American Art Collection 1930.934

Wood received his training in Minneapolis, at The Art Institute of Chicago, and later in Europe where he was greatly influenced by the work of Holbein, Dürer, and van Eyck. This portrait, supposedly of a farmer and his wife, actually represents the painter's sister and the family's local dentist. The façade of the Gothic house portrayed in the rear of the painting and the forms of the window and pitchfork are echoed in the seams of the overalls and in other elements of the composition as well. This is Grant Wood's most famous painting.

92 Ivan Le Lorraine Albright, *1897—* *American*

That Which I Should Have Done I Did Not Do, 1931–41
Oil on canvas. 97 x 36 in (246.5 x 91.5 cm)
Mary and Leigh Block Charitable Fund
Mr. and Mrs. Earle Ludgin
1955.645

Ivan Albright's wide and diverse training included The School of The Art Institute of Chicago. His incomparable sense of the surface and his fantastic interpretation of the subject set him apart from his contemporaries. Through the use of formal means, he creates a frightening world in which the commonplace is endowed with a poignant mystery. Jean Dubuffet has commented: "We feel strongly, in front of these paintings, that we live in a mirage, that our eyes, that all our vision deceives us, that all the notions on which we have until now based our standards of appreciation of all things—are erroneous."

Ivan Albright
Into the World Came a Soul Called Ida
Lithograph
Gift of Louise Lutz 1964.251

92

93

93 Salvador Dali, *1904—* *Spanish*

Inventions of the Monsters, 1937
Oil on canvas. 20⅛ x 30⅞ in (51.1 x 78.4 cm)
Joseph Winterbotham Collection 1943.798

Painted in 1937, *Inventions of the Monsters* is composed of fantastic images irrationally combined with portraits of the artist and his wife Gala. When Dali learned that the Art Institute had purchased his painting, he wired the following explanation: "Am pleased and honored by your acquisition. According to Nostradamus the apparition of monsters presages the outbreak of war. This canvas was painted in the Semmering mountains near Vienna a few months before the Anschluss and has a prophetic character. Horse women equal maternal river monsters. Flaming giraffe equals cosmic masculine apocalyptic monster. Cat angel equals divine heterosexual monster. Hourglass equals metaphysical monster. Gala and Dali equal sentimental monster. The little blue dog alone is not a true monster. Sincerely, Salvador Dali."

94 Max Beckmann, *1884–1950* *German*

Self Portrait, 1937
Oil on canvas. 75¾ x 35 in (192.5 x 88.9 cm)
Gift of Philip Ringer 1955.822

Beckmann was the greatest exponent of the Expressionist style, the German equivalent of the French Fauves, though he himself objected to such a label. Here he is at his prime, in a self portrait painted the year he emigrated from Germany—a major painter at the height of his power. The face he presents is quizzical, sardonic, and demanding. It is a brilliant painting, a near life-sized image that seems to be forged in iron.

95 Balthus (Balthasar Klossowsky), *1910—* *French*

Patience, 1943
Oil on canvas. 63⅜ x 64½ in (161.0 x 163.9 cm)
Joseph Winterbotham Collection 1964.177

Balthus, long-time director of the French Academy, Rome, is one of the enigmatic realist painters of the twentieth century. Balthus stylistically owes much to Felix Vallaton as well as to the early works of the younger Boutet de Monvel. But he early developed his own repertory and mythology of adolescent females, who seem to live an introspective life entirely their own and show the choreographic grace of young awkwardness.

Balthus: *Head of a Young Girl,* pencil
The Worcester Sketch Fund 1966.63

95

96 Edward Hopper, *1882–1967* *American*

Nighthawks, 1942
Oil on canvas. 33 3/16 x 60 1/8 in (84.3 x 152.7 cm)
Friends of American Art Collection 1942.51

Edward Hopper studied in New York under Henri and Kenneth Hayes Miller, and later spent a year in Paris. He painted pictures of American urban places—houses, motels, lunch counters. His works reflect a feeling of nostalgia and loneliness for the America of his youth. In *Nighthawks* the vivid colors of the intensely lighted interior are pitted against the strong dark tones of the exterior. The result is powerful and arresting, and yet all elements in the painting are always skillfully balanced.

96

97

[97] René Magritte, *1898–1967* *Belgian*

Time Transfixed, 1939
Oil on canvas. 57½ x 38⅜ in (146.1 x 97.5 cm)
Joseph Winterbotham Collection 1970.426

Magritte has been both claimed and disclaimed by the Surrealists. But, like the artistic revolutionaries, he does use traditional symbols to upset traditional relationships. "If the spectator finds," the artist wrote, "that my paintings are a kind of defiance of 'common sense,' he realizes something obvious. I want nevertheless to add that for me the world is a defiance of common sense."

[98] Willem de Kooning, *1904—* *American*

Excavation, 1950
Oil on canvas. 80⅛ x 100⅛ in (203.5 x 254.3 cm)
Mr. and Mrs. Frank G. Logan Purchase Prize, Gift of
Mr. Edgar Kaufmann, Jr., and Mr. and Mrs. Noah Goldowsky 1952.1

The Dutch-born de Kooning emigrated to America in 1926 and emerged as one of its dominant painters after his first solo exhibition in 1948. The viewer of *Excavation* is barraged by images—and is given no help in sorting them out. De Kooning writes: "The attitude that nature is chaotic and that the artist put order into it is a very absurd point of view. I think all we can hope for is to put some order into ourselves. When a man plows his field at the right time, it means just that."

98

99 Jackson Pollock, *1912–56* *American*

Grayed Rainbow, 1953
Oil on canvas. 72 x 96 in (182.9 x 244.0 cm)
Gift of the Society for Contemporary Art
1955.494

Working with huge canvases directly on the floor, Pollock evolved the unconventional method that he used in this painting: dripping paint (often aluminum paint and enamel mixed with sand, glass, and other foreign matter) onto the surface of his picture. His work may be thought of in relation to landscape or the movement of the stars; yet it has no reference to objects that exist, or to ideal forms. "My paintings do not have a center," Pollock wrote. They "depend on the same amount of interest throughout."

99

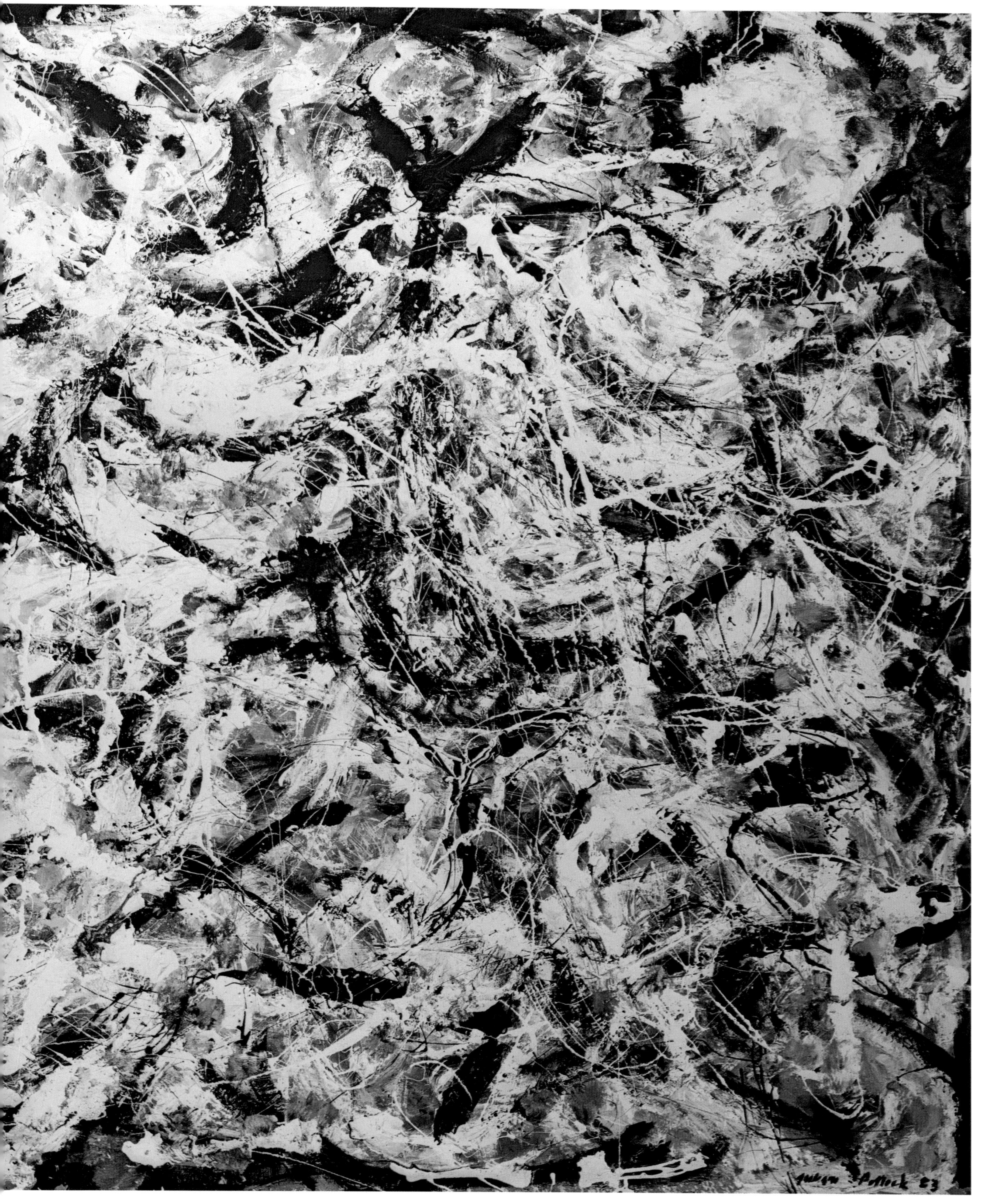

100

100 Frank Stella, *1936—* *American*

De La Nada Vida A La Nada Muerte, 1965
Metallic paint on canvas. 81 x 293 in (205.7 x 744.2 cm)
Ada S. Garrett Prize Fund 1966.335

Since the beginning of his career Frank Stella has produced innovative abstract paintings which he has developed in more than a dozen different series. This canvas is an outstanding piece from the "Running V" group, which represents a major achievement in his early work. Its twenty parallel horizontal stripes are painted in metallic brass paint. Scintillations of color and form give an illusion of spatial recession or projection. "The solution I arrived at—and there are probably quite a few, although I know of only one other, color density—forces illusionistic space out of the painting at a constant rate by using a regulated pattern," explains Stella.

Detail from tapestry entitled *Caesar in Battle with Women and Children.*
One of a set of fourteen known as the Cleopatra Series.
Wool and silk, tapestry weave.
Flanders, Brussels, about 1680.
Gift of Mrs. Chauncey McCormick and Mrs. Richard Ely Danielson 1944.20

Index to the Text

Fragment, Spain, thirteenth century.
Silk and linen, twill weave, in shades of red, green, and off-white.
Grace R. Smith Textile Fund. 1976.341

Index to Artists and Works